QUEUE

Reading Comprehension

8

Third Edition

by Jonathan D. Kantrowitz

Edited by Katherine Pierpont

Class Pack ISBN: 978-0-7827-1013-7 • Student Book ISBN: 978-0-7827-1007-6
Item Code QWK1088 • Copyright © 2011 Queue, Inc.

Queue, Inc. • 80 Hathaway Drive, Stratford, CT 06615
(800) 232-2224 • Fax: (800) 775-2729 • www.qworkbooks.com

Table of Contents

To the Students v

from "Trifles" *by Susan Glaspell* 1

"Future Scientist" 6

Preserving the Present:
   Time Capsules...............................11

Jumbo 18

from *Tarzan of the Apes* 21
   by Edgar Rice Burroughs

Seat Belts..24

from *The Call of the Wild* 28
   by Jack London

Communication 32

Ralph Nader 36

from *Tarzan of the Apes*
   Part II 39
   by Edgar Rice Burroughs

Kristine Lilly 42

Sengbe Pieh (Cinque)—
   Capture, Revolt and Recapture 45

The Complicated Life of a
   Patuxent Whooper Egg.................49

from *A Fancy of Hers* 52
   by Horatio Alger

from *A Fancy of Hers—*Part II............55
   by Horatio Alger

from *Peter Pan by J.M. Barrie* 60

from "Negro Schoolmaster in
   the New South" 63
   by W.E.B. DuBois

Soy Protein 65

The Captive *by John R. Musick*..........69

Harry and His Dog 73
   by Mary Russell Mitford

from *The Golden Touch*.......................78
   by Nathaniel Hawthorne

from *The Velveteen Rabbit* 83
   by Margery Williams Bianco

Cesar Chavez.....................................87

Earth's Water 90

Traveling Abroad................................93

Censorship in Music 96

from *The Financier* 102
   by Theodore Dreiser

Poison Ivy and Its Cousins 113

James P. Beckwourth, Black
   Mountain Man.............................116

African Americans in Combat 119

from *The Red-Headed League* 121
   by Arthur Conan Doyle

The Quest for Happiness 125
   FROM "DELICATESSEN"
      by Joyce Kilmer
   "YOUNG LOCHINVAR"
      by Sir Walter Scott

"Get Up and Bar the Door"................131

"The Men that Don't Fit In" 135
   by Robert W. Service

"Harriet Beecher Stowe"....................138
   by Paul Laurence Dunbar

Excerpted from "The Pied Piper of
   Hamelin, A Child's Story".............141
   by Robert Browning

from "Hiawatha's Childhood"............146
   by Henry Wadsworth Longfellow

from "The Rime of the Ancient
   Mariner" 151
   by Samuel Taylor Coleridge

"Two Moods from the Hill" 157
   by Ernest Benshimol

"The Planting of the
   Apple Tree" 160
   by William Cullen Bryant

The Delaware People 164

Captain Kidd on Raritan Bay 166

Woodrow Wilson 170

Valley Forge.....................................174

The Battle of Gettysburg 178

The Battle of Gettysburg—Part II....181

Disputes Over the Penns'
   Proprietorship 184

To the Students

Tips for Answering Multiple-Choice Questions

Multiple-choice questions have a **stem,** which is a question or incomplete sentence followed by four answer choices. You should select only one answer choice. The following are some tips to help you correctly answer multiple-choice questions:

- Read each passage carefully.
- Read each question and think about the answer. You may look back to the reading passage as often as necessary.
- Answer all questions on your answer sheet. Do not mark any answers to questions in your test booklet.
- For each question, choose the best answer and completely fill in the circle in the space provided on your answer sheet.
- If you do not know the answer to a question, skip it and go on. You may return to it later if you have time.
- If you finish the section of the test that you are working on early, you may review your answers in that section only. Don't go on to the next section of the test.

Tips for Answering Open-Ended Questions

Remember to:

- Read the question carefully. Be sure you understand it before you begin writing.
- Be sure your essay has a main idea. This should be in your introduction.
- Support your main idea with details, explanations, and examples.
- State your ideas in a clear sequence.
- Include an opening and a closing.
- Use a variety of words and vary your sentence structure.
- Check your spelling, capitalization, and punctuation.
- Write neatly.

from "TRIFLES"

by Susan Glaspell

This play involves a murder mystery. Who killed Mr. Wright? In this excerpt from the play, two men are in the Wright home, investigating the crime. The men's wives have accompanied them. As the men search for hard evidence, the women consider the subtle elements of the case and the relationship between Mr. and Mrs. Wright.

MRS. PETERS. (*Glancing around.*) Seems funny to think of a bird here. But she must have had one, or why should she have a cage? I wonder what happened to it.

MRS. HALE. I s'pose maybe the cat got it.

MRS. PETERS. No, she didn't have a cat. She's got that feeling some people have about cats—being afraid of them. My cat got in her room, and she was real upset and asked me to take it out.

MRS. HALE. My sister Bessie was like that. Queer, ain't it?

MRS. PETERS. (*Examining the cage.*) Why, look at this door. It's broke. One hinge is pulled apart.

MRS. HALE. (*Looking, too.*) Looks as if someone must have been rough with it.

MRS. PETERS. Why, yes. (*She brings the cage forward and puts it on the table.*)

MRS. HALE. I wish if they're going to find any evidence they'd be about it. I don't like this place.

MRS. PETERS. But I'm awful glad you came with me, Mrs. Hale. It would be lonesome for me sitting here alone.

MRS. HALE. It would, wouldn't it? (*Dropping her sewing.*) But I tell you what I do wish, Mrs. Peters. I wish I had come over sometimes she was here. I—(*Looking around the room.*)—wish I had.

MRS. PETERS. But of course you were awful busy, Mrs. Hale—your house and your children.

MRS. HALE. I could've come. I stayed away because it weren't cheerful—and that's why I ought to have come. I—I've never liked this place. Maybe because it's down in a hollow, and you don't see the road. I dunno what it is but it's a lonesome place and always was. I wish I had come over to see Minnie Foster[1] sometimes. I can see now—(*Shakes her head.*)

MRS. PETERS. Well, you mustn't reproach yourself, Mrs. Hale. Somehow we just don't see how it is with other folks until—something comes up.

1

MRS. HALE. Not having children makes less work—but it makes a quiet house, and Wright out to work all day, and no company when he did come in. Did you know John Wright, Mrs. Peters?

MRS. PETERS. Not to know him; I've seen him in town. They say he was a good man.

MRS. HALE. Yes—good; he didn't drink, and kept his word as well as most, I guess, and paid his debts. But he was a hard man, Mrs. Peters. Just to pass the time of day with him— (*Shivers.*) Like a raw wind that gets to the bone. (*Pauses, her eye falling on the cage.*) I should think she would 'a wanted a bird. But what do you suppose went with it?

MRS. PETERS. I don't know, unless it got sick and died. (*She reaches over and swings the broken door, swings it again, both women watch it.*)

MRS. HALE. You weren't raised round here, were you? (*Mrs. Peters shakes her head.*) You didn't know—her?

MRS. PETERS. Not till they brought her yesterday.

MRS. HALE. She—come to think of it, she was kind of like a bird herself—real sweet and pretty, but kind of timid and—fluttery. How—she—did—change. (*Silence; then as if struck by a happy thought and relieved to get back to everyday things.*) Tell you what, Mrs. Peters, why don't you take the quilt in with you? It might take up her mind.

MRS. PETERS. Why, I think that's a real nice idea, Mrs. Hale. There couldn't possible be any objection to it, could there? Now, just what would I take? I wonder if her patches are in here—and her things. (*They look in the sewing basket.*)

MRS. HALE. Here's some red. I expect this has got sewing things in it. (*Brings out a fancy box.*) What a pretty box. Looks like something somebody would give you. Maybe her scissors are in here. (*Opens box. Suddenly puts her hand to her nose.*) Why—(*Mrs. Peters bends nearer, then turns her face away.*) There's something wrapped up in this piece of silk.

MRS. PETERS. Why, this isn't her scissors.

MRS. HALE (*lifting the silk*). Oh, Mrs. Peters—it's—(*Mrs. Peters bends closer.*)

MRS. PETERS. It's the bird.

[1] **Minnie Foster** is Mrs. Wright's maiden name.

1   Read the following sentence from the story and then answer the question.

"Not having children makes less work—but it makes a quiet house, and Wright out to work all day, and no company when he did come in."

The author *probably* chooses these words to show that Mrs. Hale—

A   thinks it would have been pleasant to live in the Wright house
B   thinks people should keep their concerns to themselves
C   thinks Mrs. Wright probably led a boring and lonesome life
D   thinks Mr. Wright should have been rewarded for his hard work

Read this statement carefully and think about what the author intended the character to mean by it. Mrs. Hale probably did not mean it was pleasant in the Wright house (answer choice A). She makes a point to say that because of her concerns she probably should have visited Mrs. Wright more often (answer choice B). While she does mention that Mr. Wright works all day, she doesn't suggest he should be praised for this (answer choice D). Her statement is based on the idea that the Wright house must have been quiet and lonely. Mrs. Wright probably led a sad life. Answer choice C is best.

2   Mrs. Hale *most* likely compares Mrs. Wright with a bird to show that Mrs. Wright—

A   is pretty and timid
B   is an excellent singer
C   is proud of her appearance
D   is trapped in a small room

According to Mrs. Hale, Mrs. Wright was similar to a bird. This question asks you why Mrs. Hale made this unusual comparison. There was no mention of singing (answer choice B) in the excerpt, so this probably isn't the correct answer. Answer choice C does not seem to have anything to do with the story. Mrs. Wright did seem trapped in a small room (answer choice D) like a bird in a cage, but Mrs. Hale did not make that connection. She thinks that Mrs. Wright was like a bird because she was pretty, but often scared (answer choice A).

3 Which line from the story *best* identifies the conflict in the story?

  A "my sister Bessie was like that"
  B "my cat got in her room, and she was real upset"
  C "I wonder what happened to it"
  D "I'm awful glad you came with me, Mrs. Hale"

This question asks you which line from the story lets readers identify the conflict, or main problem, in the story. To find the main problem, look at each answer choice and then pick the one that describes a problem that the characters deal with throughout the entire story. Mrs. Hale mentions that her sister Bessie does not like cats (answer choice A), but is this problem the main problem in the story? The two women also mention that Mrs. Wright once got upset when a cat got into her room (answer choice B). Though this may seem like a conflict, it is not the main problem in the story, so answer choice B is incorrect. Mrs. Peters and Mrs. Wright spend a good deal of time discussing the fact that Mrs. Wright's bird is missing, and they question what happened to the bird (answer choice C) more than once in the story. Since this problem appears throughout the story, from beginning to end, answer choice C may be correct. Though Mrs. Peters is glad that Mrs. Hale came with her (answer choice D), the main problem in the story was not that Mrs. Peters did not want to go to Mrs. Wright's house alone. The conflict in this story is the missing bird, and it is resolved at the end of the story. Answer choice C is correct.

4 Which of the following judgments can be made about Mr. Wright?

  A He was mean and dishonest.
  B He was decent but cold to his wife.
  C He was a good friend of Mrs. Peters.
  D He gave his wife a cat as a pet.

In the story, Mrs. Hale tells Mrs. Peters about Mr. Wright. Think back to their conversation. Did Mrs. Hale suggest that he was mean and dishonest (answer choice A)? No, she said that he probably acted fairly and told the truth. Mrs. Peters said that she only knew Mr. Wright to see him, so they would not have been good friends (answer choice C). Earlier in the story, Mrs. Peters explains that Mrs. Wright did not have a cat (answer choice D). The best answer is answer choice B. Mr. Wright was a decent man, but he was not pleasant or warm to his wife.

4

5   Which word *best* describes the tone of the story?

    A   Frightening
    B   Intriguing
    C   Infuriating
    D   Fascinating

This question asks you to consider the plot and setting of the story, as well as the way that the characters' reactions to the plot and setting contribute to the tone of the story. Though we know from the beginning of the story that Mr. Wright has been murdered, the characters do not seem to feel frightened; answer choice A is probably incorrect. Because there is a mystery to be solved, both the characters and the reader are likely to feel intrigued (answer choice B). This answer choice may be correct, but before you choose answer choice B as the correct answer, read the other choices to be sure. Though the mystery of the missing bird is not solved until the end of the story, the two women are certainly not infuriated (answer choice C) by this, nor do they seem to find it particularly fascinating (answer choice D). They are more puzzled, or intrigued, by the bird's whereabouts. Answer choice B is correct.

6   Which word *best* describes Mrs. Hale and Mrs. Peters in the story?

    A   Critical
    B   Sensitive
    C   Hopeful
    D   Competitive

Think back to the story you just read. What sort of characters were Mrs. Hale and Mrs. Peters? What did they say and how did they act? They did not seem critical of Mrs. Wright (answer choice A); instead, they seemed to feel sorry for her. They were definitely sensitive to Mrs. Wright's situation (answer choice B), so this may be the correct answer. Answer choice C is not correct. They don't seem hopeful for her future. And, while they felt sorry for Mrs. Wright, they weren't in competition with her (answer choice D). Answer choice B is the best answer.

5

"FUTURE SCIENTIST"

My shelves are covered with beakers
  and slides,
My desk with a scientific text
On Newton's laws of gravity,
Which I can't wait to study next.

My locker at school is filled to the brim
With ideas for several experiments
And my book is wrapped in a cover I
  made
From the periodic table of elements.

You see, I fell for science at a very
  young age
When I planted flowers outside my
  window
Where, with plenty of sun and a
  sprinkle of rain,
They sprouted and continued to grow.

It was amazing to me that life could
  spring
From a dirt-filled terracotta pot
And from that point on my science
  book became
The only book I never forgot.

I read about seeds and leaves and cells
And roots and pollination
And how plants keep cool by releasing
  water
Through a process called transpiration.

When I finished with plants, I turned
  the page
And read about the sun, moon, and
  stars
And it wasn't long before my telescope
Was aimed toward the planet Mars.

After the solar system I studied the
  Earth
From the air to the land to the seas
And learned about rocks and how
  mountains form
And why the polar ice caps might
  unfreeze.

I discovered that plates within Earth's
  crust
Slide along, get stuck, and then break
And cause the ground to tremble and
  roll
And create a giant earthquake.

The next unit I studied was all about
  genes,
And not the kind that you wear,
But rather the ones that determine the
  look
Of your nose and your eyes and your
  hair.

I learned about the musculoskeletal
  system,
The bones that help us stand up
  straight
And the muscles that offer the
  strength that we need
To run, jump, swim, and *ambulate*.

Blood, I read, is pumped by the heart
Into vessels called arteries
And reaches tissues and organs
Through the walls of capillaries.

Curie, Einstein, Watson, Crick,[1]
And other scientific giants
Are not only the heroes that I adore,
But the developers of modern science.

Their discoveries have kept me reading
Through my science book
And have made me pause a time or
  two
To have a second look.

Because of them I'll keep on reading
So my love for this subject endures
And maybe one day I'll be a scientist,
  too,
And find new species, planets, or cures.

[1] Marie **Curie**—made advances in radiation; Albert
Einstein—discovered the theory of relativity; James
Watson and Francis **Crick**—figured out the structure
of DNA

1   The speaker of the poem *first* began studying science because—

   A   he watched plants grow in pots of dirt
   B   he read a book about Albert Einstein
   C   he was fascinated by the solar system
   D   he learned a lot about science in school

The speaker talks about many of his scientific studies in the poem. However, a single one started his passion for science. Think about which event made him become interested in science. There is no mention of a book about Einstein (answer choice B), and the speaker's fascination with the solar system (answer choice C) did not begin until after he had started studying science. The speaker does study science in school (answer choice D), but he says that he actually started "at a very young age" when he watched plants grow. Answer choice A is correct.

2   What is the meaning of *ambulate* as used in the poem?

   A   Walk
   B   Drink
   C   Pass
   D   Read

This question asks you to use the context of lines from the poem to determine the meaning of an unknown word. Read the lines carefully. Think about the words that come before the unknown word. What do these words have in common? They are all action words that deal with the ways in which people move. They do not talk about drinking (answer choice B), and nothing is being passed (answer choice C) in this line. Although the speaker does a lot of reading (answer choice D) this line deals more with muscles and movement. The best answer is answer choice A. The word meanings match well: run, jump, swim, and walk.

7

3 Which of these does the speaker use to cover his science book?

   A Diagrams of the planets
   B Pages from other books
   C Pictures of his scientific heroes
   D The periodic table of elements

This question asks you to recall a detail from the poem. Think back to where the speaker talks about the cover he made for his science book. What made this cover special? While he did study planets, the cover was not a diagram of them (answer choice A). There is no mention of other books that he might have used (answer choice B). The speaker does talk about scientist heroes, but he doesn't talk about having pictures of them (answer choice C). However, he does say that he uses a periodic table to make a book cover (answer choice D).

4 Which word *best* describes the speaker in the poem?

   A Careless
   B Intrigued
   C Foolish
   D Concerned

Think about the speaker of the poem. Whether or not you realized it, by reading his words you've learned a lot about what kind of a person he is. Does he seem careless (answer choice A)? Not really, he seems to put a lot of care into what he is doing. Is he intrigued (answer choice B). He is. Is he foolish (answer choice C)? No, he seems to be a sensible person. Answer choice B is the best answer. He might be concerned about science (answer choice D), but he's definitely excited and intrigued by it.

5   Explain how the speaker's interest in science began and how it grew as he learned more? Be sure to write your response in your answer document.

This question asks about the causes and effects of the speaker's passion for science. To answer this question, you'll need to write one or more paragraphs. You can look back to the poem to find all the information you need to write your answer. Think about what first causes the speaker's interest, and then trace his development as he learns about new topics. Finally, tell what he hopes to accomplish with all of his learning.

Sample answer:

In the poem, the speaker first becomes involved with science when he plants some flowers in pots of dirt. When he watches them grow, he becomes fascinated by plants and begins to read about them in his science book. After that, he moves on to another chapter, this one about the solar system. Then, he reads about the features of Earth, and finally about the human body. After all of his study, he has found heroes in scientists like Curie and Einstein and he wants to become a scientist as well.

_____

_____

_____

_____

_____

_____

_____

_____

_____

_____

_____

_____

_____

_____

PRESERVING THE PRESENT: TIME CAPSULES

PEOPLE OF THE PRESENT know about past cultures from discoveries of documents and artifacts that have been either accidentally or intentionally preserved. Archaeologists[1] and anthropologists[2] have dedicated countless hours to unearthing and restoring these artifacts in order to piece together the history of humankind. Consider how much easier this job would be today if past peoples had had the *foresight* to create time capsules to aid our understanding of their cultures.

A time capsule is a container that holds documents and objects that represent a culture at a certain point in time. Time capsules are designed to enable future generations to view the preserved artifacts and documents to help them understand the cultural elements of past societies.

The first large-scale time capsule was created by the Westinghouse Electric Corporation and displayed at the 1939 World's Fair in New York City, an event that allowed companies from all over the world to exhibit their newest and greatest ideas and inventions. Engineers at the corporation were challenged to create a vessel that would be able to preserve its contents for thousands of years. These engineers designed a material called Cupaloy that was as strong as steel and as resistant to corrosion as copper.

The 800-pound, missile-shaped vessel was then filled with a very thick glass tube containing about 35 objects specially chosen by a committee to represent life at that time, including a dollar bill, a baseball, a fountain pen, eyeglasses, a wristwatch, a toothbrush, a deck of cards, and a Mickey Mouse cup.

The committee also decided to include a variety of seeds, fabrics, metals, and other manufactured materials that they thought might not exist in the distant future. In addition, a reel of microfilm containing text from newspapers, magazines, and books was also preserved in order to present future peoples with an ample understanding of life in the 1930s. While the project was interesting and entertaining, it also suggests that people understood how quickly the world was changing and how different things would be in the future.

On September 28, 1938, the capsule was lowered into an underground, glass-lined chamber in Flushing Meadows Park, located in Queens, New York. A document called the *Book of Record* was then created to allow people of the future to find and unearth the capsule 5,000 years later. It contains a detailed description of the burial site and the contents of the capsule, as well as a key to the English language in case it is no longer used in the year 6939. About 3,000 copies of the *Book of Record* were printed on special paper using ink that is designed to last throughout time. These copies were then distributed to libraries and archival collections all over the world.

In 1965, after recognizing the rapid development of society since the first time capsule had been buried, Westinghouse created a second time capsule to document these drastic changes. This second capsule contains items such as a credit card, a record by the musical group The Beatles, a ballpoint pen, contact lenses, an electronic watch, an electric toothbrush, and a transistor radio, as well as newly developed medicines and scientific instruments. This second time capsule was buried beside the first. The site is marked with a concrete pillar that explains what lies beneath.

Since the idea first originated, many people have created their own time capsules to preserve elements of their personal lives. Today, the Internet makes it possible for people all over the world to document where their time capsules are buried so that future peoples can find them. Though no one can be sure that this method of preserving history will be effective, it will most likely enable people of the future to understand more than we are presently able to about our ancestors.

[1]**archaeologist**: scientist who studies the material remains of past human life and activities

[2]**anthropologist**: scientist who studies the origins and social elements of human cultures, past and present

1   The author *most* likely wrote the first paragraph to—

    A   tell how people of the past might have lived
    B   show how archeologists teach us about the past
    C   show that time capsules help us remember the past
    D   tell the history of humankind up to the present century

This question asks you to decide what the main idea of the first paragraph is. All of the answer choices are mentioned, but only one is the focus of the whole paragraph. The paragraph does talk about people of the past, but it does not talk about how they might have lived. They are only mentioned in reference to something else (answer choice A). Though the entire article is about time capsules, this paragraph does not mention them until the final sentence, so answer choice C is incorrect. The paragraph talks about how people of the present learn about the history of humankind, but this is not the focus of the first paragraph. The paragraph is mostly about how we learn about people in the past, which is through the work of archeologists. Answer choice B is correct.

2 Which would *best* provide information about the locations of different time capsules around the world?

    A A dictionary
    B Encyclopedias
    C An atlas
    D Web sites

This question asks you to decide which reference source would be the best one to consult if you wanted to know more about where different time capsules all over the world are buried. A dictionary (answer choice A) might provide you with the definition of a time capsule, but it would not contain the information you were looking for. Encyclopedias (answer choice B) are good sources of historical information, but most likely would not contain the locations of different time capsules around the world. An atlas (answer choice C) is full of maps and geographical information. You could use it to look up a country in which you already know a time capsule us buried, but the atlas itself would not give you this information. Web sites (answer choice D) would tell you all about the different time capsules that people have created, as well as where they are buried and what they contain. Answer choice D is correct.

3 What is the meaning of *foresight* as used in the article?

    A Ability
    B Respect
    C Thought
    D Tools

This question asks you to figure out the meaning of a word from the context of the sentence. We don't know if past people were able to make time capsules, so answer choice A isn't the best. Making time capsules does not necessarily have anything to do with respect, so answer choice B also is not correct. As the reader learns, time capsules can be very simple devices that don't always require special tools (answer choice D). The best answer is answer choice C—we're sorry that past people hadn't thought to make time capsules for us.

4   Which of these *best* describes why Westinghouse buried a second time capsule?

    A   To ensure that at least one would be found
    B   To include microfilm containing text from books
    C   To display it at the World's Fair in New York City
    D   To show that society had developed very quickly

You can find the answer to this question in the article. Reread the paragraph discussing the second time capsule. Answer choice A is not correct, because this detail isn't mentioned in the article. And the first time capsule contained microfilm, so answer choice B is not the correct answer. Answer choice C is also not correct. The second time capsule wasn't created to display at the World's Fair. Answer choice D is the correct answer.

5   The author *most* likely wrote this article to—

    A   convince readers to buy time capsules
    B   explain the development of the first time capsule
    C   entertain with a story about making a time capsule
    D   inform readers about two large time capsules

This question asks about the main purpose of the article. To answer this question, think about what the author is trying to communicate to the reader by writing this article. The article isn't persuasive (answer choice A). It discusses more than just the first time capsule, so answer choice B is not the best answer. It is not a story meant to entertain (answer choice C). However, it does inform readers about two very large time capsules (answer choice D). Answer choice D is the best answer.

14

6 Which of the following judgments can be made about what will *most* likely happen next?

   A People of the future will use the **Book of Record** to find the time capsule.
   B Each item in the time capsule will be removed when people don't use it anymore.
   C The *Book of Record* will provide people with text from 1930s books and papers.
   D Future peoples will not be very interested in the stories of the past.

This question asks you to predict what will probably happen based on what you've read. The answer to this question is not directly stated in the article, but you can infer the answer from what is stated. The author states that the Book of Record was created to allow the people of the future to find and unearth the capsule 5,000 years later; this idea is described in answer choice A. The article does not state that things will be removed from the capsule (answer choice B), so this is not the correct answer. Answer choice C is incorrect because the text from 1930s books and newspapers was put onto microfilm and buried inside of the capsule; it was not contained in the Book of Record. The time capsule is a way to get future peoples interested in the past, so answer choice D is not the best prediction. Answer choice A is the best answer.

15

7 What sorts of items were included in the time capsules? Why does the author *most* likely list these items in the article? Be sure to write your response in your answer document.

This is a short-response question. You have to write out your answer to this question. Think about the items of each time capsule and why the author might have chosen to list those specific items. What was her purpose for including this information?

Sample answer:

The author lists the contents of the time capsules for two reasons. First, she wants readers to understand the kinds of items that were chosen to represent life in the 1930s, as well as the type of items that might be included in a time capsule. Second, she is illustrating how much societal change took place between the burial of the first and second time capsules. While the first contained a dollar bill, the second contained a credit card. A fountain pen was included in the first, and a ballpoint pen was included in the second. The first held a pair of eyeglasses, while the second held a pair of contact lenses. The author is trying to get readers to understand how much society advanced in this short amount of time. She may also be encouraging readers to consider how much society could advance in 5,000 years, when the first time capsule is scheduled to be unearthed.

_____

_____

_____

_____

_____

_____

_____

_____

_____

_____

_____

JUMBO

Jumbo was an African bull elephant. He spent the first two decades of his life in captivity at England's London Zoo. He gave rides to thousands of children.

Jumbo was over 20 years old by the time he gained international attention, when he joined P.T. Barnum's circus in 1882. Jumbo came to symbolize the meaning of "big."

Jumbo was a small, scrawny baby elephant when he was captured in Central Africa. He was lovingly cared for, fed, groomed and trained by his keeper, Matthew Scott. He weighed an estimated seven tons and stood nearly 12 feet tall by the time Barnum sought to purchase him.

The London Zoological Society feared that the huge animal might one day become a danger to the public. Barnum's offer of $10,000 was readily accepted. However, English citizens from Queen Victoria to the man in the street protested the potential loss of what had become a national treasure.

Barnum delighted in the "Jumbo-mania" that raged between the two countries. He gained what he loved most—free publicity. Eventually, he refused to reconsider the deal. He transported Jumbo and Scott to America on board a huge freighter. The *Assyrian Monarch* sailed on a 15-day voyage across the Atlantic.

On Easter Sunday, 1882, Jumbo arrived at a dock in New York City. Thousands greeted him. Over the next three years, Jumbo was *the focal point* of the Barnum and Bailey Circus. He was viewed by an estimated 20 million people.

Jumbo died on September 15, 1885, in Canada. He was struck by a freight train. As with many things related to Barnum, stories vary about Jumbo's demise. Some say that he deliberately stood firm in the train's path. Others say that he had been attempting to protect a younger elephant named "Tom Thumb."

Barnum was determined to continue using Jumbo as an attraction. He contracted with a taxidermy firm to rebuild the giant elephant. His skin, weighing an estimated 1,500 pounds, was stretched over a large wooden model. The "restored" Jumbo continued to appear with the circus for several years.

Eventually, Barnum donated Jumbo's skeleton of more than 2,000 bones to the American Museum of Natural History in New York. He donated the mounted hide to Tufts University. It remained there until it was destroyed by fire in 1975.

Matthew Scott, Jumbo's longtime friend and trainer, was devastated by Jumbo's demise. He went on to care for small animals at the Barnum and Bailey Circus' winter headquarters in Bridgeport, Connecticut.

1 The author *most* likely uses the words *the focal point* to show that Jumbo became—

   A the largest thing
   B the main attraction
   C a frequent visitor
   D a famous animal

2 Why did the London Zoological Society sell Jumbo?

   A They thought he might be dangerous.
   B They needed to get money for their zoo.
   C They wanted him to be in a circus.
   D They could no longer afford to feed him.

3 The author *most* likely wrote this article to—

   A persuade readers of an elephant's importance
   B inform readers about an elephant's life
   C tell a story about famous animals
   D explain the development of a circus

4 Why was Jumbo taken to New York City?

   A He was going to give rides to children.
   B He needed to be with Matthew Scott.
   C He had been struck by a freight train.
   D He had been sold to a new owner.

19

5 Why do you think Tufts University kept Jumbo's hide? Be sure to write your response in your answer document.

_____

_____

_____

_____

_____

_____

_____

_____

_____

_____

_____

_____

_____

_____

_____

_____

_____

_____

_____

_____

_____

_____

from "TARZAN OF THE APES" – Part I

by Edgar Rice Burroughs

From early childhood he had used his hands to swing from branch to branch after the manner of his giant mother. As he grew older he spent hour upon hour daily speeding through the treetops with his brothers and sisters.

He could spring twenty feet across space at the dizzy heights of the forest top, and grasp with unerring precision, and without apparent jar, a limb waving wildly in the path of an approaching tornado.

He could drop twenty feet at a stretch from limb to limb in rapid descent to the ground, or he could gain the utmost pinnacle of the loftiest tropical giant with the ease and swiftness of a squirrel.

Though but ten years old he was fully as strong as the average man of thirty. He was far more agile than the most practiced athlete ever becomes. And day by day his strength was increasing.

His life among these fierce apes had been happy. His recollection held no other life, nor did he know that there existed within the universe aught else than his little forest and the wild jungle animals with which he was familiar.

He was nearly ten before he commenced to realize that a great difference existed between himself and his fellows. His little body, burned brown by exposure, suddenly caused him feelings of intense shame, for he realized that it was entirely hairless, like some low snake, or other reptile.

He attempted to obviate this by plastering himself from head to foot with mud, but this dried and fell off. Besides it felt so uncomfortable that he quickly decided that he preferred the shame to the discomfort.

In the higher land which his tribe frequented was a little lake. It was here that Tarzan first saw his face in the clear, still waters of its bosom.

It was on a sultry day of the dry season that he and one of his cousins had gone down to the bank to drink. As they leaned over, both little faces were mirrored on the placid pool; the fierce and terrible features of the ape beside those of the aristocratic scion of an old English house.

Tarzan was appalled. It had been bad enough to be hairless, but to own such a countenance! He wondered that the other apes could look at him at all.

That tiny slit of a mouth and those puny white teeth! How they looked beside the mighty lips and powerful fangs of his more fortunate brothers!

21

And the little pinched nose of his; so thin was it that it looked half starved. He turned red as he compared it with the beautiful broad nostrils of his companion. Such a generous nose!

Why it spread half across his face! "It certainly must be fine to be so handsome," thought poor little Tarzan.

But when he saw his own eyes; ah, that was the final blow—a brown spot, a gray circle and then blank whiteness! Frightful! Not even the snakes had such hideous eyes as he.

1   Why was Tarzan ashamed of his appearance?

    A   He was covered with mud.
    B   Other people made fun of his looks.
    C   Members of his family were unattractive.
    D   He looked so different from the apes.

2   What is this story *mostly* about?

    A   How apes swing on vines
    B   What apes look like
    C   A man who lives among apes
    D   A family of apes in the jungle

22

3 What do Tarzan's ashamed feelings about himself suggest about how humans measure their own beauty and self-worth? Be sure to write your response in your answer document.

_____

_____

_____

_____

_____

_____

_____

_____

_____

_____

_____

_____

_____

_____

_____

_____

_____

_____

_____

_____

_____

_____

_____

23

SEAT BELTS

Did you know that seat belts are the most effective means of reducing fatalities and serious injuries in a traffic crash? It's true. In fact, seat belts save over 10,000 lives in America every year.

The sad fact is that thousands of people still die in traffic crashes every year. When a vehicle is involved in a crash, passengers are still traveling at the vehicle's original speed at the moment of impact. When the vehicle finally comes to a complete stop, unbelted passengers slam into the steering wheel, windshield, or another part of the vehicle's interior. (Ouch!)

Seat belts are your best protection in a crash. They are designed so that the strongest areas of your body absorb the forces in a crash. Those are the areas along the bones of your hips, shoulders, and chest. The belts keep you in place so that your head, face, and chest are less likely to strike the windshield, dashboard, other vehicle interiors, or other passengers. They also keep you from being thrown out of a vehicle.

The Top Four Reasons Why You Should Wear Your Seat Belt:

- Seat belts can save your life in a crash.
- Seat belts can reduce your risk of a serious injury in a crash.
- Thousands of the people who die in car crashes each year might still be alive if they had been wearing their seat belts.
- It's easy. It only takes three seconds.

What's the right way to wear your safety belt? The lap belt or lap portion of the lap/shoulder belt should be adjusted so that it is low and snug across the pelvis/lap area—never across the stomach. The shoulder belt should cross the chest and collarbone and be snug. The belt should never cross the front of the face or be placed behind your back.

The adult lap and shoulder belt will fit you properly when you can sit with your back against the vehicle seat back cushion, with knees bent over the vehicle seat edge and feet on the floor. So, to wear seat belts, you must be at least 4'8" tall and weigh about 80 pounds.

If the lap and shoulder belt do not fit you right now, you should be using a belt-positioning booster seat! A booster seat raises your sitting height, which enables the lap and shoulder belt to fit you properly.

How Seat Belts Can Stop You in a Crash

One-tenth of a second after impact, the motor vehicle comes to a stop. The unbelted occupant slams into the car's interior. Immediately after the unbelted occupant stops moving, his internal organs collide with each other and also with skeletal systems. To allow the occupant to come to a more gradual stop, all the stopping distance must be used.

Holding you in your seat with a safety belt allows you to stop as the car is stopping, thereby enabling you to "ride down" the crash.

During a crash, safety belts distribute the forces of rapid deceleration over larger and stronger parts of the body such as the chest, hips, and shoulders. Additionally, the safety belt actually stretches slightly to slow down and to increase its stopping distance. The head, face, and chest are also less likely to strike the steering wheel, windshield, dashboard, or the car's interior frame.

People wearing safety belts are not thrown into another person or ejected from the vehicle. Also, the safety belt helps belted drivers maintain control of the car by keeping them in the driver's seat. This increases the chance of preventing a second crash.

Seat Belts and Air Bags

You still must buckle your seat belt even if you're riding in a car with an air bag. Air bags can cause injuries or even death when people are too close at the time of *deployment*. Everyone should sit at least 10 inches away from where the air bag is stored. Young children who are riding in child safety seats or older children who are riding in booster seats should ride in the back seat, furthest away from an air bag. In fact, children 12 years of age and under should always be properly buckled up in the back seat!

Front seat driver and passenger side air bags only work in frontal crashes, so if your car is hit on the side or rolls over, the air bag will not protect you—only your seat belt, when worn properly, can do that!

Using Seat Belts with Child Safety Seats

Securing newborns and toddlers in child safety seats is known to reduce the chances of serious injury in a crash. Each child under the age of 12 should be buckled into her or his appropriate seat: the vehicle's back seat or a child safety seat in the back of the car. Newborns should be placed in rear-facing car seats in the back seat.

1 The author *most* likely includes the bullets under the fourth paragraph to—

    A organize information so it's easily understood

    B draw the reader's attention to important points

    C tell what the author will discuss next

    D reinforce important points stated in the article

2 What is the function of a booster seat?

    A To protect kids from air bags

    B To replace the use of a seat belt

    C To make a seat belt fit properly

    D To keep kids in the back seat

3 What is the meaning of the word *deployment* as used in this article?

    A Stops working

    B Requires fixing

    C Goes into use

    D Crashes into cars

4 According to the selection, is a seat belt or an air bag more important for crash safety? Be sure to write your response in your answer document.

27

from "THE CALL OF THE WILD"
by Jack London

Buck had accepted the rope with quiet dignity. To be sure, it was an unwonted performance but he had learned to trust in men he knew, and to give them credit for a wisdom that outreached his own. But when the ends of the rope were placed in the stranger's hands, he growled menacingly. He had merely intimated his displeasure, in his pride believing that to intimate was to command. But to his surprise the rope tightened around his neck, shutting off his breath. In a quick rage he sprang at the man, who met him halfway, grappled him close by the throat, and with a deft twist threw him over on his back. Then the rope tightened mercilessly, while Buck struggled in a fury, his tongue lolling out of his mouth and his great chest panting futilely. Never in all his life had he been so vilely treated, and never in all his life had he been so angry. But his strength ebbed, his eyes glazed, and he knew nothing when the train was flagged and the two men threw him into the baggage car.

The next he knew, he was dimly aware that his tongue was hurting and that he was being jolted along in some kind of a conveyance. The hoarse shriek of a locomotive whistling a crossing told him where he was. He had traveled too often with the Judge not to know the sensation of riding in a baggage car. He opened his eyes, and into them came the unbridled anger of a kidnapped king. The man sprang for his throat, but Buck was too quick for him. His jaws closed on the hand, nor did they relax till his senses were choked out of him once more.

"Yep, has fits," the man said, hiding his mangled hand from the baggage man, who had been attracted by the sounds of struggle. "I'm taking him up for the boss to 'Frisco. A crack dog doctor there thinks that he can cure him."

Concerning that night's ride, the man spoke most eloquently for himself, in a little shed back of a saloon on the San Francisco waterfront.

"All I get is fifty for it," he grumbled, "and I wouldn't do it over for a thousand, cold cash."

His hand was wrapped in a bloody handkerchief, and the right trouser leg was ripped from knee to ankle.

"How much did the other mug get?" the saloon-keeper demanded.

"A hundred," was the reply. "Wouldn't take a sou less, so help me."

"That makes a hundred and fifty," the saloon-keeper calculated, "and he's worth it, or I'm a squarehead."

The kidnapper undid the bloody wrappings and looked at his lacerated hand. "If I don't get hydrophobia—"

"It'll be because you was born to hang," laughed the saloon-keeper. "Here, lend me a hand before you pull your freight," he added.

Dazed, suffering *intolerable* pain from throat and tongue, with the life half throttled out of him, Buck attempted to face his tormentors. But he was thrown down and choked repeatedly, till they succeeded in filing the heavy brass collar from off his neck. Then the rope was removed, and he was flung into a cage-like crate.

1   Why did the man put a rope around Buck's neck?

   A   Because the man hated dogs
   B   Because Buck was a wild dog
   C   Because the man wanted to capture Buck
   D   Because the man was afraid to go near Buck

2   Buck realizes that he is on a locomotive when he —

   A   hears the baggage man talking
   B   hears a whistle blowing
   C   is put into a cage
   D   hears the wheels turning

3   What is the meaning of the word *intolerable* as used in the story?

   A   Wonderful
   B   Strange
   C   Terrible
   D   Imagined

4   What will *most* likely happen to Buck next?

   A   Buck will give up fighting.
   B   Buck will be taken to a doctor.
   C   Buck will escape from the man.
   D   Buck will be let go in the woods.

5 Which word *best* describes how Buck feels when he wakes up in the baggage car?

- **A** Furious
- **B** Scared
- **C** Confused
- **D** Obedient

6 Think about the characters and events in this story. Around which period in history do you think this story takes place? Be sure to write your response in your answer document.

_____

_____

_____

_____

_____

_____

_____

_____

_____

_____

_____

_____

_____

_____

_____

_____

_____

_____

30

31

COMMUNICATION

Ever hear the story of the couple who, on the eve of their fiftieth anniversary, sat down for a snack? With makings for a sandwich before him, the husband reached into a new bag of bread and handed his wife the heel. She then burst out, "For fifty years you have been giving me the heel. I won't take it anymore! When will you think of me for a change?"

"But, Honey," he replied with shock, "I gave you my favorite part!"

Communication *snafus* happen in the best of relationships. Sometimes the solution is as simple as asking questions to ensure that you have understood your partner accurately.

There are many ways of communicating in a relationship. Some will be productive and move each of you to a higher level of understanding about each other. Some will not. Learning how to communicate effectively is a skill that takes practice. It is important to recognize poor communication styles. Once you recognize them you can begin to repair them.

A passive communication style is one in which someone is not honestly identifying his or her feelings. This is the "martyr syndrome." The passive communicator risks being treated like a doormat. Another style is an aggressive style of communication. This individual tries to communicate through intimidation. Unfortunately, this style of communication is also ineffective. It usually makes people defensive. Another dysfunctional style of communication is a passive-aggressive style. This person presents as passive or benign on the surface. However, in hidden, underhanded ways she or he sets out to undermine or diminish another individual.

Communication is not a contest. It's not like a debate, where there is one winner. Rather, the best result is a "win-win" situation where both parties achieve a better understanding of the other's feelings. Communication is a skill that can be learned. A key component is active listening.

An effective listener doesn't force the speaker to do all the work. He or she enters into the process. Be patient with pauses. Don't rush a speaker who seems to be blocked momentarily. Rather, feed back a few of the last words spoken or feelings expressed. Keep an open mind. Before disagreeing, make sure that you've fully comprehended what was said. Both partners get to practice expressing their own feelings in a given situation, allowing the other adequate opportunity to present ideas, too. Ask for clarification if any point is confusing. Try not to be defensive. Rather than preparing a *retort*, really listen to what the other person is saying. Acknowledge feelings, rather than attributing them to the other party.

Expressing what you feel and need to a partner is very important. So much of the time, we expect our partner to "know what we need" without having to say it. This is an unreasonable expectation. It often leads to serious disappointments and feelings of inadequacy.

32

- I feel . . .
- I need for you to . . .
- I am willing to . . .
- What do you need from me?

Practicing this exchange can lead to a better understanding of what each of you is really expecting and hoping for in the relationship.

1 Why does the author tell the anecdote about the old couple in the *first* paragraph?

A To show what happens when couples are passive-aggressive
B To prove that it is important to express your feelings
C To show the importance of good communication
D To prove that it is important to be kind

2 What is the meaning of *snafus* as used in the article?

A Examples
B Blunders
C Types
D Insults

3 From information in this selection, the reader can conclude that one trait of a good listener is—

A finishing the speaker's sentences during pauses
B making sure the message is understood
C letting the speaker do all of the work
D waiting for the speaker to come to you

4 What is the meaning of *retort* as used in this article?

    A Resolve

    B Joke

    C Pause

    D Reply

5 Why does the author begin the first paragraph with a question?

    A To get the reader's attention

    B To make the reader aware of a problem

    C To teach an important lesson

    D To reach an important conclusion

6 Briefly explain two examples of good communication and two examples of bad communication. Be sure to write your response in your answer document.

_____

_____

_____

_____

_____

_____

_____

_____

_____

_____

_____

_____

_____

_____

RALPH NADER

Ralph Nader was born in 1934 in the small factory town of Winsted, Connecticut. His parents were proud Lebanese immigrants. His father, Nathra Nader, ran the Highland Arms Restaurant in town. He engaged his customers in spirited debate about public affairs.

As a child, Ralph was studious, bright, and intense. His parents challenged and inspired their four children—two sons and two daughters—to think for themselves, to have opinions, and to stand up for what they believed was right. They even took their children to town government meetings to learn what it truly meant when one person spoke out.

Ralph played with David Halberstam, the future journalist, when they were both young boys. He also read back issues of the *Congressional Record*. By the age of 14, he had read the early "muckrakers." They inspired his thinking about the distribution of power in American society. He graduated *magna cum laude* from Princeton in 1955. In 1958, he graduated from Harvard Law School.

It was at Harvard that Ralph first explored an unorthodox legal topic: the engineering design of automobiles. He was concerned about safety. He knew that there were five million automobile accidents reported every year. These accidents caused nearly 40,000 fatalities, 110,000 permanent disabilities, and 1.5 million injuries annually.

His research resulted in an April 1959 article, published in *The Nation*. It was called "The Safe Car You Can't Buy." In this article, Ralph declared, "Detroit is designing automobiles for style, cost and performance. Cars are not designed for safety."

In 1963, Ralph was an unknown 29-year-old attorney. He decided to change his life. He abandoned a law practice in Hartford, Connecticut. He hitchhiked to Washington, D.C. There he began a long life of professional citizenship.

"I had one suitcase," he recalled. "I stayed in the YMCA. Walked across a little street and had a hot dog, my last." A few years later, he would expose the *repulsive* ingredients that go into hot dogs.

Ralph took a job as a consultant to the U.S. Department of Labor. He worked for Assistant Secretary of Labor Daniel Patrick Moynihan. He moonlighted as a freelance writer for *The Nation*. He also wrote for *The Christian Science Monitor*. He acted as an unpaid adviser to a Senate subcommittee. The subcommittee was exploring the role that the federal government might play in auto safety.

In 1965, armed with a wealth of research and a passion for the topic, Ralph targeted General Motors (GM) and the American auto industry. His bestselling book was called *Unsafe at Any Speed: The Designed-In Dangers of the American Automobile.* Using all sorts of immoral and underhanded tactics, GM attempted to discredit him. He then sued them for invasion of privacy. This landmark case forced the president of GM to go before a Senate committee. He had to admit that GM had behaved improperly. The money Ralph received when the case was settled was the most ever received for a lawsuit of this type. A series of safety laws was passed in 1966. These laws forced the auto industry to make drastic design changes so that motor vehicles would be safer. With the money Ralph had won in the settlement, he launched the modern consumer movement.

Ralph Nader continues to speak out today, calling attention to the situations and the practices that he and his "Nader's Raiders" believe to be questionable or wrong. He has run three times for the office of president of the United States, once in 1996, again in 2000, and then in 2004. His campaigns have brought significant attention to his message and to his political party at the time, the Green Party. Ralph Nader has never forgotten his humble roots, however, as he describes them in his memoir, *The Seventeen Traditions*, published in January 2007.

1   Why did the author *most* likely write this passage?

   A   To show how cars have become safer over the years
   B   To persuade readers to give up hot dogs and hamburgers
   C   To describe what it is like to attend Harvard Law School
   D   To inform readers about a man who has helped consumers

2   Which of these statements is *best* supported by the passage?

   A   Ralph Nader hated going to his classes.
   B   Ralph Nader helped the car companies.
   C   Ralph Nader wanted to help people.
   D   Ralph Nader dreamed of being rich.

3   What is the meaning of *repulsive* as used in this article?

   A   Significant
   B   Disgusting
   C   Ridiculous
   D   Nutritional

4 How did Ralph Nader change his life?

    A He went back to school.
    B He started working at Harvard.
    C He abandoned his law practice.
    D He sued a car magazine.

5 What do you think the modern consumer movement involves? Be sure to write your response in your answer document.

_____

_____

_____

_____

_____

_____

_____

_____

_____

_____

_____

_____

_____

_____

_____

_____

_____

_____

_____

from "TARZAN OF THE APES" – Part II

by Edgar Rice Burroughs

He did not hear the parting of the tall grass behind him as a great body pushed itself stealthily through the jungle. Nor did his companion, the ape, hear either, for he was drinking. The noise of his sucking lips and gurgles of satisfaction drowned the quiet approach of the intruder.

Not thirty paces behind the two she crouched—Sabor, the huge lioness—lashing her tail. Cautiously she moved a great padded paw forward, noiselessly placing it before she lifted the next. Thus she advanced; her belly low, almost touching the surface of the ground—a great cat preparing to spring upon its prey.

Now she was within ten feet of the two unsuspecting little playfellows. Carefully she drew her hind feet well up beneath her body, the great muscles rolling under the beautiful skin. So low she was crouching now that she seemed flattened to the earth except for the upward bend of the glossy back as it gathered for the spring. No longer the tail lashed. Quiet and straight behind her it lay.

An instant she paused thus, as though turned to stone, and then, with an awful scream, she sprang.

Sabor, the lioness, was a wise hunter. To one less wise the wild alarm of her fierce cry as she sprang would have seemed a foolish thing, for could she not more surely have fallen upon her victims had she but quietly leaped without that loud shriek?

But Sabor knew well the wondrous quickness of the jungle folk and their almost unbelievable powers of hearing. To them the sudden scraping of one blade of grass across another was as effectual a warning as her loudest cry. Sabor knew that she could not make that mighty leap without a little noise.

Her wild scream was not a warning. It was voiced to freeze her poor victims in a paralysis of terror for the tiny fraction of an instant which would suffice for her mighty claws to sink into their soft flesh and hold them beyond hope of escape.

So far as the ape was concerned, Sabor reasoned correctly. The little fellow crouched trembling just an instant, but that instant was quite long enough to prove his undoing.

Not so, however, with Tarzan, the man-child. His life amidst the dangers of the jungle had taught him to meet emergencies with self-confidence, and his higher intelligence resulted in a quickness of mental action far beyond the powers of the apes.

So the scream of Sabor, the lioness, *galvanized* the brain and muscles of little Tarzan into instant action.

Before him lay the deep waters of the little lake, behind him certain death; a cruel death beneath tearing claws and rending fangs.

39

1 Sabor screams loudly before she leaps to—

    A warn her victims of danger
    B alert other animals of her presence
    C scare her victims so they don't move
    D give her victims a chance to get away

2 Which of these *best* describes the tone of the story?

    A Joyful
    B Tense
    C Considerate
    D Encouraging

3 What is the meaning of *galvanized* as used in the story?

    A Pointed
    B Brightened
    C Programmed
    D Jolted

4 Which of these describes what Tarzan will *most* likely do next?

    A He will try to find some help.
    B He will go back to fight Sabor.
    C He will go back to save the ape.
    D He will look for a hiding place.

5 Explain why Tarzan fled after the ape was attacked. Be sure to write your response in your answer document.

_____

_____

_____

_____

_____

_____

_____

_____

_____

_____

_____

_____

_____

_____

_____

_____

_____

_____

_____

_____

_____

_____

_____

KRISTINE LILLY

Kristine Marie Lilly was born in New York City on July 22, 1971. She grew up in Wilton, Connecticut. At a young age, she quickly became an excellent soccer player. When she was a student at Wilton High School, Kristine's team won state soccer titles during her freshman, sophomore, and senior years. She served as team captain as a junior and senior.

While still a high school student, Kristine debuted for the national women's soccer team. Kristine's debut performance was during the sixteenth match ever played by the U.S. Women's team. The date was August 3, 1987. At the age of 16 years and 12 days, she was the second youngest player ever to don a U.S. jersey. Mia Hamm, her teammate, was the youngest.

Kristine attended the University of North Carolina (UNC), where she was a four-time first selection All-American. She was twice named the "Most Valuable Player" (MVP) of the NCAA Championship. She helped to lead UNC to four NCAA championships from 1989–1992. Kristine completed her collegiate career with 78 goals and 41 assists.

Kristine's junior year in college proved to be very rewarding. She won the 1991 Hermann Trophy as the best female college soccer player in America. She was also a finalist for the Broderick Award as the outstanding female athlete in all of college sports. She was the second-leading scorer in the nation with 15 goals and four assists. Mia Hamm was first. In December of 1993, Kristine graduated from UNC with a degree in communications. Just one year later, her UNC number (15) was retired.

After college, Kristine Lilly went on to help the USA win two Women's World Cups and numerous international tournaments. She scored three pivotal goals during the 1996 Olympic games, earning the team the gold medal. In 1999, Kristine led the National Team with twenty goals and played a *crucial* role in the World Cup final game against China. She cleared a Chinese shot off the goal line with her head in sudden death overtime. She also nailed the third penalty kick resulting in a U.S. win, 5–4. Kristine was named MVP of the U.S. Women's Cup in 1999. She was an All-Tournament selection in 1995, 1996, and 1997.

On January 18, 2006, Kristine earned her 300th cap for the U.S. Women's team in a game against Norway. A cap is a recognition earned by a player for each appearance in an international game for his or her country. She is the first player in soccer history, man or woman, to reach that milestone. She is tied with Michelle Akers for second place on the team's all-time goal scoring list with 105.

Kristine has played for nearly 20 years on the national team. The left-footed, left-sided mid-fielder has established herself as one of the top players in the world. Her hometown of Wilton, Connecticut, dedicated a day to her and honored her with a parade after she won the gold medal. A road sign entering the town reads, "Welcome to Wilton: Hometown of Olympic Gold Medalist Kristine Lilly." Kristine runs the Kristine Lilly Soccer Academy every summer in Wilton. Following the Women's World Cup victory, the Wilton High School soccer field was named after her.

1　The author *most* likely wrote this article to—

    A　describe the final match of a the Women's World Cup
    B　tell readers about a talented, interesting soccer player
    C　explain how to start a soccer league in your school
    D　introduce readers to the women of the National Soccer Team

2　What is the meaning of *crucial* as used in the article?

    A　Important
    B　Painful
    C　Honorary
    D　Colorful

3　Which of these awards did Kristine Lilly win in 1991?

    A　The U.S. Women's Cup MVP
    B　The Broderick Award
    C　The Hermann Trophy
    D　The Wilton High School title

4　Which of the following judgments can be made about Kristine Lilly?

    A　She is not as good as Mia Hamm.
    B　She is an incredibly talented athlete.
    C　She didn't work very hard in school.
    D　She is not popular in her hometown.

43

5 Describe the important ideas you would use if you were going to give a talk to your class about Kristine Lilly. Be sure to write your response in your answer document.

_____

_____

_____

_____

_____

_____

_____

_____

_____

_____

_____

_____

_____

_____

_____

_____

_____

_____

_____

_____

_____

_____

44

SENGBE PIEH (CINQUE)
CAPTURE, REVOLT, AND RECAPTURE

THE CAPTURE

Sengbe Pieh was born about 1813. He was the son of a local chief. He was born in the town of Mani in Upper Mende country. It was ten days' march from the Atlantic coast. Sengbe became a farmer and got married; he and his wife had a son and two daughters.

One day in late January 1839, he was going to his field. He was captured in a surprise attack by four men. He was taken to a nearby village to a man called Mayagilalo. After three days, Mayagilalo gave Sengbe over to a local king, King Siaka, in payment of a debt. After staying in Siaka's town for a month, Sengbe was marched to Lomboko, a notorious slave-trading island. He was sold to the richest slaver there, the Spaniard Pedro Blanco, whose activities had helped to make King Siaka wealthy as well.

At Lomboko, Sengbe was imprisoned with other slaves. More slaves joined them for the two months they were there. They all were waiting to be transported across the Atlantic. Most of the captives came from Mende country. Some, who did not speak Mende, learned the language during their forced journey through Mende country to the coast. Most were farmers. Others were hunters and blacksmiths. This is surprising because all over West Africa, blacksmiths held a sacred place in society and could neither be enslaved nor killed even during war.

All these people were shipped from Lomboko in March aboard the schooner *Tecora*, which arrived at Havana in the Spanish colony of Cuba in June. At a slave auction following an advertisement, Jose Ruiz, a Spanish plantation owner, bought Sengbe and 48 others for $450 each to work on his sugar plantation at Puerto Principe, another Cuban port three hundred miles from Havana. Pedro Montez, another Spaniard bound for the same port, bought three girls and a boy.

On June 26th, the 53 Africans were herded on board an American-built schooner. It had originally been called *Friendship*, but was changed to the Spanish *La Amistad* when the vessel changed ownership and was registered as a Spanish subject.

THE REVOLT

The trip to Puerto Principe usually took three days, but the winds were *adverse*. Three days out at sea, on June 30th, Sengbe used a loose spike that he had removed from the deck to unshackle himself and his fellow slaves. They had been whipped and maltreated and, at one point, made to believe that they would be killed for supper on arrival. Sengbe armed himself and the others with cane knives found in the cargo hold. He then led them on deck, where they killed Captain Ferrer and the cook Celestino and wounded the Spaniard Montez. Sengbe spared Montez's life along with those of Ruiz and Antonio, the cabin boy. The mutineers lost two of their own party, killed by Captain Ferrer. Two white seamen managed to escape from the *Amistad* in a small boat.

45

Sengbe then ordered the Spaniards to sail in the direction of the rising of the sun, or eastward towards Africa. At night, however, Montez, who had some experience as a sailor, navigated by the stars and sailed westward. He was hoping to remain in Cuban waters. Nevertheless, a gale drove the ship northeasterly along the United States coastline. The schooner followed a zigzag course for two months, during which time eight more slaves died of thirst and exposure. Sengbe held command the whole time, forcing the others to conserve food and water, and allotting a full ration only to the four children. He took the smallest portion for himself.

RECAPTURE

The *Amistad* drifted off Long Island, New York, in late August 1839. Sengbe and others went ashore to trade for food and supplies and to negotiate with local seamen to take them back to Africa. News soon got around about a mysterious ship in the neighborhood with her "sails nearly all blown to pieces." It was the "long, low, black schooner," the story of which had been appearing in newspapers in previous weeks as the ship cruised in a northeastern direction along the U.S. coastline. Reports said that Cuban slaves had revolted and killed the crew of a Spanish ship and were roaming the Atlantic as buccaneers.

On August 26th, the United States survey brig *Washington* sighted the battered schooner near Culloden Point on the eastern tip of Long Island. The United States Navy and the Customs Service had previously issued orders for the capture of the ship.

When the *Amistad* was captured, a reporter from the *New York Sun* witnessed Sengbe's defiance of and repeated attempts to escape from his captors. Sengbe jumped overboard. He had to be dragged back onto the ship. He urged his fellow slaves to fight against hopeless odds. He was taken away to the American vessel and separated from his men. He made such a violent protest that the naval officers allowed him to remain on the *Washington*'s deck, where he stood and stared fixedly at the *Amistad* throughout the night.

1   What is Sengbe Pieh's *main* conflict in the story?

    A His friends were arrested by the navy.
    B He had been hurt and lost in another country.
    C His ship was lost in the Atlantic Ocean.
    D He was captured and forced into slavery.

2   What is the meaning of *adverse* as used in the story?

    A Refreshing
    B Unfavorable
    C Frightening
    D Nonexistent

3   Which of the following judgments can be made about Sengbe?

    A He didn't care about other people.
    B He desperately wanted to go home.
    C He was an excellent navy captain.
    D He didn't think about his actions.

4   The author *most* likely wrote this story to—

    A tell about a brave man forced into slavery
    B inform readers about the plight of the *Amistad*
    C challenge beliefs about Sengbe and his crew
    D describe what it was like to be forced into slavery

5   The author *most* likely includes the information in the seventh paragraph to—

    A show how badly Sengbe was treated
    B show what happened to the ship
    C explain why Sengbe liked Montez
    D explain why the ship was renamed

6 Which of these describes what will *most* likely happen next?

    A Sengbe will be set free.
    B Sengbe will try to escape.
    C The navy will hire Sengbe.
    D The ship will finally sink.

7 Write a paragraph that could have appeared in Sengbe's journal. Be sure to write your response in your answer document.

_____

_____

_____

_____

_____

_____

_____

_____

_____

_____

_____

_____

_____

_____

_____

_____

_____

_____

_____

48

THE COMPLICATED LIFE OF A PATUXENT WHOOPER EGG

In nature, whooping cranes usually mate, establish territory, build a nest, and then lay two eggs. If everything goes right, they will raise one chick. Life for the Patuxent whooper cranes—and for the people who care for them—is more complicated.

At the U.S. Geological Survey's Patuxent Wildlife Research Center, whoopers usually mate, establish territory in their pen, build a nest, and then lay two eggs, which is called a "clutch." However, the birds don't get to keep these eggs. After they lay the second egg, we remove the clutch. Why? Because removing the clutch after it has been laid causes the cranes to lay again in about 10 days. By taking the eggs away, we can increase production by three or four times. So instead of only laying two eggs and raising at the most one chick, as they would in the wild, Patuxent's whoopers may lay six or eight eggs each year. The whoopers are usually allowed to incubate their last egg and raise the chick themselves.

What happens to all the other eggs? Whooper eggs do best if incubated by cranes instead of by mechanical incubators, at least in the early stages. Every time we remove an egg, we take it to the propagation building, carrying it in a rigid suitcase redesigned to be a portable incubator. The eggs are handled carefully, since jostling them and temperature extremes can kill a fragile embryo. At the propagation building, the eggs are weighed, measured, and examined to make sure that they are not cracked or have weak shells. (Eggs with cracks or thin shells will have to receive special care if we hope to hatch a chick from them.)

We give each egg an identification number based on the parent's pen location and the order in which the egg was laid. This number is written directly on the egg's shell with a lab marker. After this is done, we bring the egg back to the crane pens and place it under an incubating sandhill crane for the next 10 days.

Patuxent maintains a flock of Florida and greater sandhill cranes, both for incubating whooper eggs and for providing non-endangered birds to use in studies. Pairs of sandhill cranes are rated, based on previous years' breeding experience, on their incubation and parenting skills. Only the highest-rated pairs are trusted with whooper eggs. Detailed charts are kept on each pair's breeding schedule—when they laid their own eggs and how long they've been incubating—so that the birds will be ready when we give them a whooper egg.

The surrogate sandhills will incubate the whooper egg for ten days. Both the male and the female will take turns caring for it. After 10 days, we'll remove it, take it back to the propagation building, and weigh and examine it again to see if it's fertile. Weighing it also tells us if the egg has lost too much weight. A fertile egg is a living thing. All fertile eggs lose weight as the chick inside grows and uses up the egg's material. However, excessive weight loss indicates that the egg is dehydrating too quickly. We often remedy problems like this, since the egg weight is critical.

49

If the egg is fertile and healthy, flock manager Jane will check the charts to decide which pair of sandhills would be best to incubate the egg for the next 10 days. After those 20 days, the whooper egg will be brought in again to make sure that it is developing normally. At 20 days, it is safe to place the egg in a mechanical incubator for the last ten days of incubation.

Managing the care of whooper eggs means knowing what stage of incubation they're at, what condition they're in and, most importantly, where they are. At the height of the breeding season, there might be over 50 whooper eggs and over 100 sandhill eggs to keep track of. Since all crane eggs look similar, proper identification of each individual egg and careful record-keeping is critical. Even if we're in a hurry—and in the breeding season, we're always in a hurry—paperwork must be done precisely and on time.

1 Patuxent whooper crane eggs are *first* incubated by—

    A a mechanical incubator
    B Patuxent whooper crane parents
    C pairs of sandhill cranes
    D a propagation building

2 The author *most* likely wrote this article to—

    A encourage readers to learn more about how eggs hatch
    B tell readers about the dangers that whooper cranes face
    C inform readers about the life of whooper crane eggs
    D give readers information about raising whooper cranes

3 Which word *best* describes the sandhill crane pairs that are given Patuxent eggs?

    A Intelligent
    B Friendly
    C Responsible
    D Elderly

4 When whoopers have completed their year's egg production, they usually—

    A raise one chick themselves
    B raise two chicks themselves
    C are given an identification number
    D incubate sandhill crane eggs

5 What are the most important elements of proper whooper egg care? Be sure to write your response in your answer document.

from "A FANCY OF HERS" – Part I

by Horatio Alger

The new school teacher was sitting at the window in her room, supper being over, when the landlady came up to inform her that Squire Hadley had called to see her.

"He is the chairman of the School Committee, isn't he?" asked the stranger.

"Yes, miss."

"Then will you be kind enough to tell him that I will be down directly?"

Squire Hadley was sitting in a rocking chair in the stiff hotel parlor, when Miss Frost entered, and said composedly, "Mr. Hadley, I believe?"

She exhibited more self-possession than might have been expected of one in her position, in the presence of official importance. There was not the slightest trace of nervousness in her manner, though she was aware that the *portly* person before her was to examine into her qualifications for the post she sought.

"I apprehend," said Squire Hadley, in a tone of dignity which he always put on when he addressed teachers, "I apprehend that you are Miss Mabel Frost."

"You are quite right, sir. I apprehend," she added, with a slight smile, "that you are the chairman of the School Committee."

"You apprehend correctly, Miss Frost. It affords me great pleasure to welcome you to Granville."

"You are very kind," said Mabel Frost demurely.

"It is a responsible, office—ahem!—that of instructor of youth," said the Squire, with labored gravity.

"I hope I appreciate it."

"Have you ever—ahem!—taught before?

"This will be my first school."

"This—ahem!—is against you, but I trust you may succeed."

"I trust so, sir."

"You will have to pass an examination in the studies you are to teach—before ME," said the Squire.

"I hope you may find me competent," said Mabel modestly,

"I hope so, Miss Frost; my examination will be searching. I feel it my duty to the town to be very strict."

"Would you like to examine me now, Mr. Hadley?"

"No," said the Squire hastily, "no, no—I haven't my papers with me. I will trouble you to come to my house tomorrow morning, at nine o'clock, if convenient."

"Certainly, sir. May I ask where your house is?"

"My boy shall call for you in the morning."

"Thank you."

Mabel spoke as if this terminated the colloquy, but Squire Hadley had something more to say.

"I think we have said nothing about your wages, Miss Frost," he remarked.

"You can pay me whatever is usual," said Mabel, with apparent indifference.

"We have usually paid seven dollars a week."

"That will be quite satisfactory, sir."

Soon after Squire Hadley had left the hotel Mabel Frost went slowly up to her room.

"So I am to earn seven dollars a week," she said to herself. "This is wealth indeed!"

1   Which word *best* describes Squire Hadley?

    A Relaxed
    B Dignified
    C Friendly
    D Informal

2   What is the meaning of *portly* as used in the story?

    A Nervous
    B Hiding
    C Stout
    D Conceited

3   Which word *best* describes how Mabel felt about the whole encounter?

    A Intimidated
    B Amused
    C Upset
    D Strange

from "A FANCY OF HERS" – Part II
by Horatio Alger

In the evening Allan Thorpe called and invited Mabel to go out for a walk. It was a beautiful moonlight night. They walked slowly to the pond, which was not far away, and sat down on a rustic seat beneath a wide spreading oak. They had been talking on various things for some time, when a sudden silence came upon both. It was at length broken by the young artist.

"I hope you will forgive me for bringing you here," he said.

"Why should you want forgiveness?" she asked, very much surprised.

"Because I brought you here with a special object in view. Rebuke me if you will, but—Mabel, I love you."

She did not seem much surprised.

"How long has it been so?" she asked in a low voice.

"I began to love you," he answered, "when I first saw you at the artists' reception. But you were so far removed from me that I did not dare to avow it, even to myself. You were a rich social queen, and I was a poor man. I should never have dared to tell you all this if you had not lost your wealth."

"Does this make me any more worthy?" asked Mabel, smiling.

"It has brought you nearer to me. When I saw how bravely you met adverse fortune; when I saw a girl brought up to every luxury, as you were, quietly devoting herself to teaching a village school, I rejoiced. I admired you more than ever, and I resolved to win you if possible. Can you give me a hope, Mabel?"

He bent over her with a look of tender affection in his manly face.

"I won't keep you in suspense, Allan," she said with an answering look. "I have not known you long but long enough to trust my future in your hands."

After a while Allan Thorpe began to discuss his plans and hopes for the future.

"I am beginning to be successful," he said. "I can, even now, support you in a modest way, and with health I feel assured of a larger—I hope a much larger—income in time. I can relieve you from teaching at once."

Mabel smiled.

"But suppose I do not consider it a burden. Suppose I like it."

55

"Then you can teach me."

"It might become monotonous to have only one pupil."

"I hope not," said Allan earnestly.

When he pressed her to name an early day for their marriage, Mabel said: "Before we go any further, I have a confession to make. I hope it won't be disagreeable to you."

He silently inclined his head to listen.

"Who told you I had lost my property?" she asked.

"No one. I inferred it from finding you here, teaching a village school for seven dollars a week," replied Allan.

"What! Have you inquired my income so exactly? I fear you are mercenary."

"I can remember the time—not so long since, either—when I earned less than that by my art. But, Mabel, what do you mean by your questions? Of course you have lost your property."

"Then my banker has failed to inform me of it. No, Allan, I am no poorer than I ever was."

"Why, then, did you become a teacher?" asked Allan Thorpe, bewildered.

"Because I wished to be of some service to my kind; because I was tired of the hollow frivolity of the fashionable world. I don't regret my experiment. I never expected to be so richly rewarded."

"And you, as rich as ever, bestow your hand on a poor artist?" he exclaimed almost incredulously.

"Unless the poor artist withdraws his offer," she answered with a smile.

1 Mabel became a teacher at a village school because—

    A she wanted to meet people
    B she wanted to help people
    C she hoped to marry
    D she needed the money

2 Which of these *best* describes why Allan Thorpe "dared" to announce his love to Mabel?

    A He admired her courageous spirit.
    B He knew she had immense wealth.
    C He believed she lost her money.
    D He thought she was beautiful.

3 Why did Allan Thorpe bring Mabel to the pond?

    A To see the moonlight
    B To show her a piece of artwork
    C To discuss her wealth
    D To declare his love

4 Which word *best* describes Allan Thorpe?

    A Relaxed
    B Rowdy
    C Wealthy
    D Humble

5 Mabel said that she had found something lacking in her previous life. If the author had added a section on what Mabel did *not* like about her earlier life, what would *most* likely be included? Be sure to write your response in your answer document.

_____

_____

_____

_____

_____

_____

_____

_____

_____

_____

_____

_____

_____

_____

_____

_____

_____

_____

_____

_____

_____

_____

6 In what ways do you think Mabel was "richly rewarded"? Be sure to write your response in your answer document.

_____

_____

_____

_____

_____

_____

_____

_____

_____

_____

_____

_____

_____

_____

_____

_____

_____

_____

_____

_____

_____

_____

from "PETER PAN"

by J.M. Barrie

Mrs. Darling loved to have everything just so, and Mr. Darling had a passion for being exactly like his neighbours; so, of course, they had a nurse. As they were poor, owing to the amount of milk the children drank, this nurse was a prim Newfoundland dog, called Nana, who had belonged to no one in particular until the Darlings engaged her. She had always thought children important, however. The Darlings had become acquainted with her in Kensington Gardens, where she spent most of her spare time peeping into perambulators, and was much hated by careless nursemaids, whom she followed to their homes and complained of to their mistresses.

She proved to be quite a treasure of a nurse. How thorough she was at bath-time, and up at any moment of the night if one of her charges made the slightest cry. Of course her kennel was in the nursery. She had a genius for knowing when a cough is a thing to have no patience with and when it needs a stocking around your throat. She believed to her last day in old-fashioned remedies like rhubarb leaf, and made sounds of contempt over all this new-fangled talk about germs, and so on. It was a lesson in propriety to see her escorting the children to school, walking sedately by their side when they were well behaved, and butting them back into line if they strayed. On John's footer days she never once forgot his sweater, and she usually carried an umbrella in her mouth in case of rain.

There is a room in the basement of Miss Fulsom's school where the nurses wait. They sat on forms, while Nana lay on the floor, but that was the only difference. They affected to ignore her as of an inferior social status to themselves, and she despised their light talk. She resented visits to the nursery from Mrs. Darling's friends, but if they did come she first whipped off Michael's pinafore and put him into the one with blue braiding, and smoothed out Wendy and made a dash at John's hair.

No nursery could possibly have been conducted more correctly, and Mr. Darling knew it, yet he sometimes wondered uneasily whether the neighbours talked.

He had his position in the city to consider.

Nana also troubled him in another way. He had sometimes a feeling that she did not admire him. "I know she admires you tremendously, George," Mrs. Darling would assure him, and then she would sign to the children to be specially nice to father. Lovely dances followed, in which the only other servant, Liza, was sometimes allowed to join. Such a midget she looked in her long skirt and maid's cap, though she had sworn, when engaged, that she would never see ten again. The gaiety of those romps! And gayest of all was Mrs. Darling, who would pirouette so wildly that all you could see of her was the kiss, and then if you had dashed at her you might have got it. There never was a simpler happier family until the coming of Peter Pan.

60

1   Which of these *best* describes Mr. Darling's problem in the middle of the story?

   A   He is worried about his reputation.
   B   He is worried about his family.
   C   He is worried about his children.
   D   He is worried about his finances.

2   Which of these *best* describes Liza?

   A   Fairly young
   B   Very pretty
   C   Hostile to Nana
   D   Well paid

3   Which of these *best* describes the tone of the story?

   A   Serious
   B   Humorous
   C   Sarcastic
   D   Argumentative

61

5 Imagine that you were going to write a reference letter for Nana. Be sure to write your response in your answer document.

_____

_____

_____

_____

_____

_____

_____

_____

_____

_____

_____

_____

_____

_____

_____

_____

_____

_____

_____

_____

_____

_____

from "NEGRO SCHOOLMASTER IN THE NEW SOUTH"

by W.E.B. DuBois

ONCE upon a time I taught school in the hills of Tennessee, where the broad dark vale of the Mississippi begins to roll and crumple to greet the Alleghenies. I was a Fisk student then, and all Fisk men think that Tennessee—beyond the Veil[1]—is theirs alone, and in vacation time they sally forth in lusty bands to meet the county school commissioners. Young and happy, I too went, and I shall not soon forget that summer, ten years ago.

First, there was a teachers' institute at the county-seat; and there distinguished guests of the superintendent taught the teachers fractions and spelling and other mysteries—white teachers in the morning, Negroes at night. A picnic now and then, and a supper, and the rough world was softened by laughter and song. I remember how—but I wander.

There came a day when all the teachers left the Institute, and began the hunt for schools. I learn from hearsay (for my mother was mortally afraid of firearms) that the hunting of ducks and bears and men is wonderfully interesting, but I am sure that the man who has never hunted a country school has something to learn of the pleasures of the chase.

I see now the white, hot roads lazily rise and fall and wind before me under the burning July sun; I feel the deep weariness of heart and limb, as ten, eight, six miles stretch relentlessly ahead; I feel my heart sink heavily as I hear again and again, "Got a teacher? Yes." So I walked on and on—horses were too expensive—until I had wandered beyond railways, beyond stage lines, to a land of "varmints" and rattlesnakes, where the coming of a stranger was an event, and men lived and died in the shadow of one blue hill.

Sprinkled over hill and dale lay cabins and farmhouses, shut out from the world by the forests and the rolling hills toward the east. There I found at last a little school. Josie told me of it; she was a thin, homely girl of twenty, with a dark brown face and thick, hard hair. I had crossed the stream at Watertown, and rested under the great willows; then I had gone to the little cabin in the lot where Josie was resting on her way to town. The gaunt farmer made me welcome, and Josie, hearing my errand, told me anxiously that they wanted a school over the hill; that but once since the war had a teacher been there; that she herself longed to learn—and thus she ran on, talking fast and loud, with much earnestness and energy . . .

I *secured* the school. I remember the day I rode horseback out to the commissioner's house, with a pleasant young white fellow, who wanted the white school. The road ran down the bed of a stream; the sun laughed and the water jingled, and we rode on. "Come in," said the commissioner—"come in. Have a seat. Yes, that certificate will do. Stay to dinner. What do you want a month?" Oh, thought I, this is lucky; but even then fell the awful shadow of the Veil, for they ate first, then I—alone.

63

¹ For DuBois, the "Veil" refers to three things. First, the Veil suggests the fact that black people have darker skin than white people do. Second, the Veil refers to the fact that white people could not see blacks as "true" Americans and as persons of equal value. Third, the Veil refers to the inability of many black people to see themselves in any other way from the way that white people saw them.

1   Which of these *best* describes the conflict in this article?

   A   The dry land in Tennessee
   B   The lack of teachers in schools
   C   The raging Mississippi River
   D   The division between races

2   What is the meaning of *secured* as used in the article?

   A   Was hired at
   B   Locked up
   C   Protected
   D   Walked past

3   Which of these *best* shows that learning is important to Josie?

   A   Josie meets Washington while going to a school in town.
   B   Josie tells Washington that her town needs a teacher.
   C   Josie spends a lot of time reading during the story.
   D   Washington finds Josie resting in the school.

64

SOY PROTEIN

Soy protein products can be good substitutes for animal products. Unlike some other beans, soy offers a "complete" protein profile. Soybeans contain all the amino acids essential to human nutrition. They must be supplied in the diet because they cannot be *synthesized* by the human body. Soy protein products can replace animal-based foods without requiring major adjustments elsewhere in the diet. Animal-based foods also have complete proteins, but tend to contain more fat, especially saturated fat.

Foreign cultures, especially Asian ones, have used soy extensively for centuries. Mainstream America has been slow to move dietary soy beyond a niche market status. In the United States, soybeans are a huge cash crop, but the product is used largely as livestock feed.

With the increased emphasis on healthy diets, this may be changing. Sales of soy products are up and are projected to increase due in part, say industry officials, to the Food & Drug Administration (FDA)–approved health claim. U.S. retail sales of soy foods were $4 billion in 2004.

Soy may seem like a new and different kind of food for many Americans. However, it actually is found in a number of products already widely consumed. For example, soybean oil accounts for 79 percent of the edible fats used annually in the United States. A glance at the ingredients for commercial mayonnaise, margarine, salad dressings, or vegetable shortening often reveals soybean oil high on the list.

These are some of the most common sources of soy protein:

- Tofu is made from cooked puréed soybeans processed into a custard-like cake. It has a neutral flavor and can be stir-fried, mixed into "smoothies," or blended into a cream cheese texture for use in dips or as a cheese substitute. It comes in firm, soft, and silken textures.

- "Soymilk," the name some marketers use for a soy beverage, is produced by grinding dehulled soybeans and mixing them with water to form a milk-like liquid. It can be consumed as a beverage or used in recipes as a substitute for cow's milk. Soymilk, sometimes fortified with calcium, comes plain or in flavors such as vanilla, chocolate, and coffee. For lactose-intolerant individuals, it can be a good replacement for dairy products.

- Soy flour is created by grinding roasted soybeans into a fine powder. The flour adds protein to baked goods and, because it adds moisture, it can be used as an egg substitute in these products. It also can be found in cereals, pancake mixes, frozen desserts, and other common foods.

- Textured soy protein is made from defatted soy flour, which is compressed and dehydrated. It can be used as a meat substitute or as filler in dishes like meatloaf.

- Tempeh is made from whole, cooked soybeans formed into a chewy cake and used as a meat substitute.

- Miso is a fermented soybean paste used for seasoning and in soup stock. Soy protein also is found in many "meat analog" products, such as soy sausages, burgers, franks, and cold cuts as well as in soy yogurts and cheese, all of which are intended as substitutes for their animal-based counterparts.

Consumers should check the labels of products to identify those most appropriate for a heart-healthy diet. Make sure the products contain enough soy protein to make a meaningful contribution to the total daily diet without being high in saturated fat and other unhealthy substances.

1   What is the meaning of *synthesized* as used in the article?

   A   Absorbed
   B   Produced
   C   Used
   D   Rejected

2   What would the author *most* likely describe if she added another paragraph?

   A   The cost of harvesting soy beans
   B   How much water soy beans require
   C   A story about working on a soy farm
   D   Special recipes using soy products

3   Soymilk is made by—

   A   mixing tofu with milk then cooking the result
   B   feeding soy to cows then letting the milk harden
   C   grinding soybeans and mixing them with water
   D   using soy to replace lactose in milk in a laboratory

4 How can soy products contribute to your health? Be sure to write your response in your answer document.

_____

_____

_____

_____

_____

_____

_____

_____

_____

_____

_____

_____

_____

_____

_____

_____

_____

_____

_____

_____

_____

_____

_____

5 Why are soybeans a "huge cash crop" in the United States if they are *not* popular in American diets? Be sure to write your response in your answer document.

_____

_____

_____

_____

_____

_____

_____

_____

_____

_____

_____

_____

_____

_____

_____

_____

_____

_____

_____

_____

_____

_____

THE CAPTIVE
from "Stories of Missouri" by John R. Musick

There is no more beautiful and thrilling tale of early pioneer days than the story of Helen Patterson. She was born in Kentucky; but while she was still a child her parents removed to St. Louis County, Missouri, and lived for a time in a settlement called Cold Water, which is in St. Ferdinand township. About the year 1808 or 1809, her father took his family to the St. Charles district, and settled only a few miles from the home of the veteran backwoodsman, Daniel Boone.

At the time of this last removal, Helen was about eighteen years of age. She was a very religious girl, and had been taught to believe that whatever she prayed for would be granted.

Shortly after the family had settled in their new home, bands of prowling savages began to roam about the neighborhood. The [American] Indians would plunder the cabins of the settlers during their absence, and drive away their cattle, horses, and hogs.

One day business called all the Patterson family to the village, except Helen. She was busily engaged in spinning, when the house was surrounded by nine [American] Indians. Resistance was useless. She did not attempt to escape or even cry out for help; for one of the savages who spoke English gave her to understand that she would be killed if she did so.

She was told that she must follow the [American] Indians. They took such things as they could conveniently carry, and with their captive set off on foot through the forest, in a northwestern direction. The shrewd girl had brought a ball of yarn with her, and from this she occasionally broke off a bit and dropped it at the side of the path, as a guide to her father and friends, who she knew would soon be in pursuit.

This came very near being fatal to Helen, for one of the [American] Indians observed what she was doing, and raised his hatchet to [harm] her. The others interceded, but the ball of yarn was taken from her, and she was closely watched lest she might resort to some other device for marking a trail.

It was early in the morning when Helen was captured. Her parents were expected to return to the cabin by noon, and she reasoned that they would be in pursuit before the [American] Indians had gone very far. As the savages were on foot, and her father would no doubt follow them on horseback, he might overtake them before dark. The uneasiness expressed by her captors during the afternoon encouraged her in the belief that her friends were in pursuit.

A little before sunset, two of the [American] Indians went back to reconnoiter, and the other seven, with the captive, continued on in the forest. Shortly after sunset, the two [American] Indians who had fallen behind joined the others, and all held a short consultation, which the white girl could not understand.

The conference lasted but a few moments, and then the savages hastened forward with Helen to a creek, where the banks were sloping, and the water shallow enough for them to wade the stream. By the time they had crossed, it was quite dark. The night was cloudy, and distant thunder could occasionally be heard.

The [American] Indians hurried their captive to a place half a mile from the ford, and there tied her with strips of deerskin to one of the low branches of an elm. Her hands were extended above her head, and her wrists were crossed and tied so tightly that she found it impossible to release them. When they had secured her to their own satisfaction, the [American] Indians left her, assuring her that they were going back to the ford to shoot her father and his companions as they crossed it.

Helen was almost frantic with fear and grief. Added to the uncertainty of her own fate was the knowledge that her father and friends were marching right into an [American] Indian *ambuscade*.

In the midst of her trouble, she did not forget her pious teaching. She prayed God to send down his angels and release her. But no angel came. In her distress, the rumbling thunders in the distance were unheard, and she hardly noticed the shower until she was drenched to the skin.

The rain thoroughly wet the strips of deerskin with which she was tied, and as they stretched she almost unconsciously slipped her hands from them. Her prayer had been answered by the rain. She hastily untied her feet, and sped away toward the creek. Guided by the lightning's friendly glare, she crossed the stream half a mile above the ford, and hastened to meet her father and friends.

At every flash of lightning she strained her eyes, hoping to catch sight of them. At last moving forms were seen in the distance, but they were too far away for her to determine whether they were white men or [American] Indians. Crouching down at the root of a tree by the path, she waited until they were within a few rods of her, and then cried in a low voice, "Father! Father!"

"That is Helen," said Mr. Patterson.

She bounded to her feet, and in a moment was at his side, telling him how she had escaped. The rescuing party was composed of her father and two brothers, a neighbor named Shultz, and Nathan and Daniel M. Boone, sons of the great pioneer, Daniel Boone.

She told them where the [American] Indians were lying in ambush, and the frontiersmen decided to surprise them. They crossed the creek on a log, and stole down to the ford, but the [American] Indians were gone. No doubt the savages had discovered the escape of the prisoner, and, knowing that their plan to surprise the white men had failed, became frightened and fled.

Helen Patterson always believed it was her prayers that saved her father, her brothers, and herself in that trying hour.

70

1 What would the author *most* likely describe if he added another paragraph?

    A Why the American Indians captured Helen
    B The adventures of the elder Daniel Boone
    C How Helen recovered from her ordeal
    D The ways people lived in pioneer days

2 What is the meaning of *ambuscade* as used in the story?

    A Trap
    B Lie
    C Shooting
    D Capture

3 What factors made Helen's escape back to her family so difficult? Be sure to write your response in your answer document.

_____

_____

_____

_____

_____

_____

_____

_____

_____

_____

_____

_____

_____

_____

_____

_____

_____

_____

_____

_____

_____

HARRY AND HIS DOG

by Mary Russell Mitford

"Beg, Frisk, beg," said little Harry, as he sat on an inverted basket, at his grandmother's door, eating, with great satisfaction, a porringer of bread and milk. His little sister Annie sat on the ground opposite to him, now twisting her flowers into garlands, and now throwing them away.

"Beg, Frisk, beg!" repeated Harry, holding a bit of bread just out of the dog's reach. The obedient Frisk squatted himself on his hind legs, and held up his forepaws, waiting for master Harry to give him the tempting morsel.

The little boy and the little dog were great friends. Frisk loved him dearly, much better than he did any one else, perhaps, because he remembered that Harry was his earliest and firmest friend during a time of great trouble.

Poor Frisk had come as a stray dog to Milton, the place where Harry lived. If he could have told his own story, it would probably have been a very pitiful one, of kicks and cuffs, of hunger and foul weather.

Certain it is, he made his appearance at the very door where Harry was now sitting, in miserable plight, wet, dirty, and half starved; and there he met Harry, who took a fancy to him, and Harry's grandmother, who drove him off with a broom.

Harry, at length, obtained permission for the little dog to remain as a sort of outdoor pensioner, and fed him with stray bones and cold potatoes, and such things as he could get for him. He also provided him with a little basket to sleep in, the very same which, turned up, afterward served Harry for a seat.

After a while, having proved his good qualities by barking away a set of pilferers, who were making an attack on the great pear tree, he was admitted into the house, and became one of its most vigilant and valued *inmates*. He could fetch or carry either by land or water; would pick up a thimble or a ball of cotton, if little Annie should happen to drop them; or take Harry's dinner to school for him with perfect honesty.

"Beg, Frisk, beg!" said Harry, and gave him, after long waiting, the expected morsel. Frisk was satisfied, but Harry was not. The little boy, though a good-humored fellow in the main, had turns of naughtiness, which were apt to last him all day, and this promised to prove one of his worst. It was a holiday, and in the afternoon his cousins, Jane and William, were to come and see him and Annie; and the pears were to be gathered, and the children were to have a treat.

Harry, in his impatience, thought the morning would never be over. He played such pranks—buffeting Frisk, cutting the curls off of Annie's doll, and finally breaking his grandmother's spectacles—that before his visitors arrived, indeed, almost immediately after dinner, he contrived to be sent to bed in disgrace.

Poor Harry! There he lay, rolling and kicking, while Jane, and William, and Annie were busy gathering the fine, mellow pears. William was up in the tree, gathering and shaking. Annie and Jane were catching them in their aprons, or picking them up from the ground, now piling them in baskets, and now eating the nicest and ripest, while Frisk was barking gaily among them, as if he were catching pears, too!

Poor Harry! He could hear all this glee and merriment through the open window, as he lay in bed. The storm of passion having subsided, there he lay weeping and disconsolate, a grievous sob bursting forth every now and then, as he heard the loud peals of childish laughter, and as he thought how he should have laughed, and how happy he should have been, had he not forfeited all his pleasure by his own bad conduct.

He wondered if Annie would not be so good-natured as to bring him a pear. All on a sudden, he heard a little foot on the stair, "pitapat," and he thought she was coming. "Pitapat" came the foot, nearer and nearer, and at last a small head peeped, half afraid, through the half-open door.

But it was not Annie's head; it was Frisk's—poor Frisk, whom Harry had been teasing all the morning, and who came into the room wagging his tail, with a great pear in his mouth; and, jumping upon the bed, he laid it in the little boy's hand.

74

1 Which word *best* describes Frisk?

    A Impatient
    B Pitiful
    C Disobedient
    D Loyal

2 Which of the following will Harry *most* likely do next?

    A He will try to be nicer to Frisk.
    B He will tell Frisk to get out of his room.
    C He will help Annie fix her doll.
    D He will follow Frisk back downstairs.

3 What is the meaning of *inmates* as used in the story?

    A Prisoners
    B Inhabitants
    C Friends
    D Children

4 What did Harry do after he cut the curls off Anne's doll?

    A He gathered pears with his cousins.
    B He played another prank on Frisk.
    C He held bread out of Frisk's reach.
    D He broke his grandmother's spectacles.

5 Which of these lines *best* identifies a conflict in the story?

   A "it was a holiday, and in the afternoon his cousins, Jane and William, were to come and see him and Annie"

   B "there he lay weeping and disconsolate, a grievous sob bursting forth every now and then, as he heard the loud peals of childish laughter"

   C "he could fetch or carry either by land or water; would pick up a thimble or a ball of cotton, if little Annie should happen to drop them"

   D "Harry, in his impatience, thought the morning would never be over"

6 This story is *mostly* about—

   A a family picking pears from a tree

   B a little boy who was sent to bed

   C a dog that is faithful to his owner

   D a girl that teases her little brother

7 Do you think that someone had told Frisk to bring Harry the pear, or that Frisk had brought it on his own? Be sure to write your response in your answer document.

_____

_____

_____

_____

_____

_____

_____

_____

_____

_____

_____

_____

_____

_____

_____

_____

_____

_____

_____

_____

_____

_____

_____

from "THE GOLDEN TOUCH"

by *Nathaniel Hawthorne*

Once upon a time, there lived a very rich man, and a king besides, whose name was Midas. He had a little daughter, whom nobody but myself ever heard of, and whose name I either never knew, or have entirely forgotten. So, because I love odd names for little girls, I choose to call her Marygold.

This King Midas was fonder of gold than of anything else in the world. He valued his royal crown chiefly because it was composed of that precious metal. If he loved anything better, or half so well, it was the one little maiden who played so merrily around her father's footstool. But the more Midas loved his daughter, the more did he desire and seek for wealth. He thought, foolish man! that the best thing he could possibly do for this dear child would be to bequeath her the largest pile of glistening coin that had ever been heaped together since the world was made.

Thus he gave all his thoughts and all his time to this one purpose. If ever he happened to gaze for an instant at the gold-tinted clouds of sunset, he wished that they were real gold, and that they could be squeezed safely into his strong box. When little Marygold ran to meet him, with a bunch of buttercups and dandelions, he used to say, "Pooh, pooh, child! If these flowers were as golden as they look, they would be worth the plucking!"

At length (as people always grow more and more foolish, unless they take care to grow wiser and wiser) Midas had got to be so exceedingly unreasonable, that he could scarcely bear to see or touch any object that was not gold. He made it his custom, therefore, to pass a large portion of every day in a dark and dreary apartment, under ground, at the basement of his palace. It was here that he kept his wealth. To this dismal hole—for it was little better than a dungeon—Midas betook himself, whenever he wanted to be particularly happy.

Here, after carefully locking the door, he would take a bag of gold coin, or a gold cup as big as a washbowl, or a heavy golden bar, or a peck measure of gold dust, and bring them from the *obscure* corners of the room into the one bright and narrow sunbeam that fell from the dungeon-like window. He valued the sunbeam for no other reason but that his treasure would not shine without its help.

And then would he reckon over the coins in the bag; toss up the bar, and catch it as it came down; sift the gold dust through his fingers; look at the funny image of his own face, as reflected in the burnished circumference of the cup; and whisper to himself, "O Midas, rich King Midas, what a happy man art thou!"

Midas was enjoying himself in his treasure room, one day, as usual, when he perceived a shadow fall over the heaps of gold. Looking up, he beheld the figure of a stranger, standing in the bright and narrow sunbeam! It was a young man, with a cheerful and ruddy face.

78

Whether it was that the imagination of King Midas threw a yellow tinge over everything, or whatever the cause might be, he could not help fancying that the smile with which the stranger regarded him had a kind of golden brightness in it.

Certainly, there was now a brighter gleam upon all the piled-up treasures than before. Even the remotest corners had their share of it, and were lighted up, when the stranger smiled, as with tips of flame and sparkles of fire.

As Midas knew that he had carefully turned the key in the lock, and that no mortal strength could possibly break into his treasure room; he, of course, concluded that his visitor must be something more than mortal.

Midas had met such beings before now, and was not sorry to meet one of them again. The stranger's aspect, indeed, was so good-humored and kindly, if not beneficent, that it would have been unreasonable to suspect him of intending any mischief. It was far more probable that he came to do Midas a favor. And what could that favor be, unless to multiply his heaps of treasure?

The stranger gazed about the room; and, when his lustrous smile had glistened upon all the golden objects that were there, he turned again to Midas.

"You are a wealthy man, friend Midas!" he observed. "I doubt whether any other four walls on earth contain so much gold as you have contrived to pile up in this room."

"I have done pretty well—pretty well," answered Midas, in a discontented tone. "But, after all, it is but a trifle, when you consider that it has taken me my whole lifetime to get it together. If one could live a thousand years, he might have time to grow rich!"

"What!" exclaimed the stranger. "Then you are not satisfied?"

Midas shook his head.

"And pray, what would satisfy you?" asked the stranger. "Merely for the curiosity of the thing, I should be glad to know."

Why did the stranger ask this question? Did he have it in his power to gratify the king's wishes? It was an odd question, to say the least.

Midas paused and meditated. He felt sure that this stranger, with such a golden luster in his good-humored smile, had come hither with both the power and the purpose of gratifying his utmost wishes. Now, therefore, was the fortunate moment, when he had but to speak, and obtain whatever possible or seemingly impossible thing, it might come into his head to ask. So he thought, and thought, and thought, and heaped up one golden mountain upon another, in his imagination, without being able to imagine them big enough.

79

At last a bright idea occurred to King Midas.

Raising his head, he looked the lustrous stranger in the face.

"Well, Midas," observed his visitor, "I see that you have at length hit upon something that will satisfy you. Tell me your wish."

"It is only this," replied Midas. "I am weary of collecting my treasures with so much trouble, and beholding the heap so diminutive, after I have done my best. I wish everything that I touch to be changed to gold!"

1   What is the meaning of *obscure* as used in this story?

   A Unseen
   B Worthless
   C Humble
   D Obvious

2   Which word *best* describes Midas?

   A Curious
   B Stubborn
   C Indifferent
   D Selfish

3   Why does the author include the second paragraph?

   A To show that King Midas loved gold and his daughter
   B To introduce the character of King Midas to readers
   C To describe for readers the size of King Midas's coin pile
   D To explain how King Midas became a powerful leader

4 Why did the author *most* likely choose the name "Marygold" for King Midas's daughter? Be sure to write your response in your answer document.

_____

_____

_____

_____

_____

_____

_____

_____

_____

_____

_____

_____

_____

_____

_____

_____

_____

_____

_____

_____

_____

_____

_____

_____

5 What do you think about King Midas's behavior and the wish he made? Be sure to write your response in your answer document.

_____

_____

_____

_____

_____

_____

_____

_____

_____

_____

_____

_____

_____

_____

_____

_____

_____

_____

_____

_____

_____

_____

_____

from "THE VELVETEEN RABBIT"

by Margery Williams Bianco

The Rabbit sighed. He thought it would be a long time before this magic called Real happened to him. He longed to become Real, to know what it felt like; and yet the idea of growing shabby and losing his eyes and whiskers was rather sad. He wished that he could become it without these uncomfortable things happening to him.

There was a person called Nana who ruled the nursery. Sometimes she took no notice of the playthings lying about, and sometimes, for no reason whatever, she went swooping about like a great wind and hustled them away in cupboards. She called this "tidying up," and the playthings all hated it, especially the tin ones.

The Rabbit didn't mind it so much, for wherever he was thrown he came down soft.

One evening, when the Boy was going to bed, he couldn't find the china dog that always slept with him. Nana was in a hurry, and it was too much trouble to hunt for china dogs at bedtime, so she simply looked about her, and seeing that the toy cupboard stood open, she made a swoop.

"Here," she said, "take your old Bunny! He'll do to sleep with you!" And she dragged the Rabbit out by one ear, and put him into the Boy's arms.

That night, and for many nights after, the Velveteen Rabbit slept in the Boy's bed. At first he found it uncomfortable, for the Boy hugged him very tight, and sometimes he rolled over on him, and sometimes he pushed him so far under the pillow that the Rabbit could scarcely breathe. And he missed, too, those long moonlight hours in the nursery, when all the house was silent, and his talks with the Skin Horse.

But very soon he grew to like it, for the Boy used to talk to him, and made nice tunnels for him under the bedclothes that he said were like the burrow the real rabbits lived in. And they had splendid games together, in whispers, when Nana had gone away to her supper and left the night-light burning on the mantelpiece. And when the Boy dropped off to sleep, the Rabbit would snuggle down close under his little warm chin and dream, with the Boy's hands clasped close round him, all night long.

And so time went on, and the little Rabbit was very happy—so happy that he never noticed how his beautiful velveteen fur was getting shabbier and shabbier, and his tail becoming unsewn, and all the pink rubbed off his nose where the Boy had kissed him.

1   What word *best* describes Rabbit at the end of the story?

    A   Worried
    B   Worn
    C   Loved
    D   Lonely

2   Why didn't Rabbit notice that he was becoming shabby?

    A   He couldn't compare himself to other toys.
    B   It was too dark to see under the covers.
    C   There were no mirrors in the bedroom.
    D   He was too happy to know what he looked like.

3   Readers can conclude that at the end of the story, Rabbit is—

    A   becoming Real
    B   being forgotten
    C   missed by the other toys
    D   lonely without his friends

4 What was happening to the Rabbit because of all of the Boy's attention? Be sure to write your response in your answer document.

_____

_____

_____

_____

_____

_____

_____

_____

_____

_____

_____

_____

_____

_____

_____

_____

_____

_____

_____

_____

_____

5 Would you want to become Real if you were the Rabbit? Be sure to write your response in your answer document.

CESAR CHAVEZ

Cesar Chavez was born in North Gila Valley, near Yuma, Arizona. He was one of six children. His parents owned a ranch and a small grocery store. During the Great Depression in the 1930s, they lost everything. In order to survive, Cesar Chavez and his family became migrant farm workers. They traveled around California to find work. It was very hard. They could not live in the same place for long. They had to follow the crops. The Chavez family would pick peas and lettuce in the winter, cherries and beans in the spring, corn and grapes in the summer, and cotton in the fall.

Working conditions for migrant workers were harsh and often unsafe. Their wages were low, and it was difficult to support a family. Cesar's family frequently did not have access to such basic needs as clean water or toilets. A large number of migrant workers were Mexican American. They also often faced prejudice. Their children had to skip school to earn wages to help support the family.

As his family moved from place to place to find work, Cesar Chavez attended about 30 schools in California. After the eighth grade, Cesar had to quit school to support his ailing parents.

Cesar's life growing up had a big impact on what he did with the rest of his life. In 1948, he married a woman who also was from a family of migrant farm workers. By 1959, the couple had eight children. Chavez, who had little education and training, was forced to return to farm work.

Cesar Chavez spent most of his life working on farms in California. Pay was low and comforts were few. He wanted to improve the situation. In the 1950s, he started organizing agricultural workers into a labor union that would demand higher pay and better working conditions from their employers. In 1962, Chavez and fellow organizer Dolores Huerta founded the Farm Workers Association.

In 1965, Chavez and Huerta agreed to honor a walkout by farm workers in Delano, California. Workers were asked not to work for the Delano grape growers. In Spanish, this strike was called a *huelga* (pronounced WELL-guh).

The strike that started in 1965 lasted for five years. It inspired a nationwide boycott of California grapes that was supported throughout the country.

There was another grape boycott in the mid-1970s. It forced growers to support the 1975 Agricultural Labor Relations Act. The United Farm Workers fought grape producers for better working conditions. Chavez and Huerta led them. They used nonviolent tactics such as protest marches, strikes, and boycotts. These tactics were usually successful. The farm workers and the growers signed agreements.

1   What was Cesar Chavez's *main* problem?

    A   His family moved around the country a lot.
    B   He felt that farm workers were treated unfairly.
    C   He had to leave school because he needed work.
    D   His father lost his farm during the Depression.

2   Which word *best* describes Cesar Chavez?

    A   Hopeless
    B   Irresponsible
    C   Inspiring
    D   Uninteresting

3   The sentence, "Cesar had to quit school to support his ailing parents" means he had to—

    A   provide for his sick parents
    B   find his parents better jobs
    C   care for his jobless parents
    D   get his parents a new home

4   What was Cesar Chavez's *main* accomplishment?

    A   Organizing a union with another person
    B   Leading several strikes against producers
    C   Having eight children in eleven years
    D   Improving conditions for migrant workers

5 Identify and explain one reason why Cesar Chavez's work was important. Be sure to write your response in your answer document.

_____

_____

_____

_____

_____

_____

_____

_____

_____

_____

_____

_____

_____

_____

_____

_____

_____

_____

_____

_____

_____

_____

_____

EARTH'S WATER

How much water is there on (and in) the earth?

As you know, the earth is a watery place. About 70 percent of the earth's surface is water-covered. Water also exists in the air as water vapor and in the ground as soil moisture and in aquifers. Thanks to the water cycle, our planet's water supply is constantly moving from one place to another and from one form to another. Things would get pretty stale without the water cycle!

When you take a look at the water around you, you see water in streams, rivers, and lakes. You see water sitting on the surface of the earth. Naturally, this water is known as "surface water." Your view of the water cycle might be that when rain falls, it fills up the rivers and lakes. However, how would you account for the flow in rivers after weeks without rain? The answer is that there is more to our water supply than just surface water. There is also plenty of water beneath our feet. It is stored in aquifers.

Even though you may only notice water on the earth's surface, there is much more water stored in the ground than there is on the surface. In fact, some of the water you see flowing in rivers comes from seepage of ground water into riverbeds. Water from precipitation continually seeps into the ground to recharge the aquifers. At the same time, water from underground aquifers continually recharges rivers through *seepage*.

People make use of both kinds of water. In the United States in 1995, we used about 321 billion gallons per day of surface water and about 77 billion gallons per day of ground water. In a way, that underestimates the importance of ground water. Not only does ground water help to keep our rivers and lakes full, it also provides water for people in places where visible water is scarce, such as in the desert towns of the western United States. Without ground water, people would be sand surfing in Palm Springs, California, instead of playing golf!

Just how much water is there on (and in) the earth? Here are some numbers you can think about. The total water supply of the world is 326 million cubic miles. If all of the world's water were poured on the United States, it would cover the land to a depth of 90 miles.

Of the fresh water on earth, much more is stored in the ground than is available in lakes and rivers. More than two million cubic miles of fresh water is stored in the earth, most within one half-mile of the surface. Contrast that with the 60,000 cubic miles of water stored as fresh water in lakes, inland seas, and rivers. If you really want to find fresh water, however, most is stored in the seven million cubic miles of water found in glaciers and ice caps, mainly in the polar regions and in Greenland.

1   This article is *mostly* about—

   A   the water supply of aquifers
   B   the water found in riverbeds
   C   the water found in glaciers
   D   the water supply of the earth

2   What is the meaning of *seepage* as used in the article?

   A   Flowing
   B   Melting
   C   Raining
   D   Drying

3   What does the author mean when he writes, "without ground water, people would be sand surfing in Palm Springs, California, instead of playing golf"?

   A   The area would be an ocean.
   B   The area would be a park.
   C   The area would be a desert.
   D   The area would be a golf course.

4 What factors affect the water supply? Why do we still experience water shortages even though the water cycle constantly recharges the water supply? Be sure to write your response in your answer document.

_____

_____

_____

_____

_____

_____

_____

_____

_____

_____

_____

_____

_____

_____

_____

_____

_____

_____

_____

_____

_____

_____

_____

92

TRAVELING ABROAD

Millions of United States citizens travel abroad each year and use their U.S. passports. When you travel abroad, the odds are in your favor that you will have a safe and incident-free trip. However, crime and violence, as well as unexpected difficulties, do befall U.S. citizens in all parts of the world. No one is better able to tell you this than U.S. consular officers. They work in the more than 250 U.S. embassies and consulates around the globe. Every day of the year, U.S. embassies and consulates receive calls from American citizens in distress.

Fortunately, most problems can be solved over the telephone or when a U.S. citizen visits the Consular Section of the nearest U.S. embassy or consulate. There are, however, less fortunate occasions when U.S. consular officers are called on to meet U.S. citizens at foreign police stations, hospitals, prisons, and even at morgues. In these cases, the assistance that consular officers can offer is specific but limited.

In the hope of helping you to avoid unhappy meetings with consular officers when you go abroad, we have prepared the following travel tips. Please have a safe trip.

❏ Safety begins when you pack. To avoid being a target, dress *conservatively*. A flashy wardrobe or one that is too casual can mark you as a tourist. As much as possible, avoid the appearance of wealth.

❏ Always try to travel light. If you do, you can move more quickly. You will be more likely to have a free hand. You will also be less tired and less likely to set your luggage down, leaving it unattended.

❏ Carry the minimum amount of valuables necessary for your trip and plan a place or places to conceal them. Your passport, cash, and credit cards are most secure when locked in a hotel safe. When you have to carry them on your person, you may wish to conceal them in several places. Avoid putting them all in one wallet or pouch. Bring travelers checks and one or two major credit cards instead of cash.

❏ Avoid handbags, fanny packs, and outside pockets, which are easy targets for thieves. Inside pockets and a sturdy shoulder bag with the strap worn across your chest are somewhat safer. One of the safest places to carry valuables is in a pouch or money belt worn under your clothing.

❏ If you wear glasses, pack an extra pair. Bring them along with any medicines you need in your carry-on luggage. To avoid problems when passing through customs, keep medicines in their original, labeled containers. Bring a copy of your prescriptions and the generic names for the drugs. If a medication is unusual or contains narcotics, carry a letter from your doctor attesting to your need to take

93

the drug. If you have any doubt about the legality of carrying a certain drug into a country, consult the embassy or consulate of that country first.

❑ Pack an extra set of passport photos along with a photocopy of your passport information page to make replacement of your passport easier in the event that it is lost or stolen.

❑ Put your name, address, and telephone number inside and outside of each piece of luggage. Use covered luggage tags to avoid casual observation of your identity or nationality and, if possible, lock your luggage.

❑ Consider getting a telephone calling card. It is a convenient way of keeping in touch. If you have one, verify that you can use it from your overseas location(s). Access numbers to U.S. operators are published in many international newspapers. Find out your access number before you go.

1   What is the meaning of *conservatively* as used in the article?

   A   Elegantly
   B   Sharply
   C   Properly
   D   Modestly

2   The author *most* likely wrote this article to—

   A   show travelers the steps they can take to keep themselves safe
   B   explain why travelers should wear their most comfortable clothes
   C   tell travelers why they should never bring any medications overseas
   D   warn travelers that there is little help for those who travel overseas

3   Preparing for having a safe trip abroad begins when you—

   A   get to the airport
   B   get on the plane
   C   land overseas
   D   start packing

94

4 Based on the information in the article, what kind of problems could you encounter while traveling? To whom can you turn for help? Be sure to write your response in your answer document.

_____

_____

_____

_____

_____

_____

_____

_____

_____

_____

_____

_____

_____

_____

_____

_____

_____

_____

_____

_____

_____

_____

CENSORSHIP IN MUSIC

Censorship in music is a topic that has brought about much controversy in the past few decades. Some people believe that music should be censored so that it will not be offensive to anyone. Others feel that music should never be subject to censorship since it is an expression of artistic creativity. Still others fall somewhere in between, opining that at least the most obscene and offensive material should be restricted in some way.

Whether or not a person finds a piece of music obscene depends largely on his or her moral or religious beliefs. These views change from generation to generation. Those people who believe that music should be censored feel that some of the language music artists use is vulgar and crude. They further this opinion by pointing out that some of this music is played on the radio and on television; therefore, it is accessible to the public.

Many parents do not wish for their children to hear foul language. Today, foul language which might be played on public radio broadcasts and on television is edited out in some way. Some artists make two versions of their songs: one uncensored for the album, and another censored for television and radio. Even cable television, which is paid for by the viewers monthly, is subject to this form of censorship, although pay-per-view-type channels are not.

Preventing or punishing speech is a clear violation of the First Amendment, which says: "Congress shall make no law *abridging* the freedom of speech or of the press." Therefore, the First Amendment guarantees the right to freedom of speech. Censorship violates this right, which is the complaint made by many musicians. Some artists express their feelings directly through their music, projecting their emotions for the world to hear. By censoring their true words and forcing them to modify their lyrics, censors in essence limit the artist's right to express himself or herself.

Does censoring music really solve the problem of exposing children to explicit language? Many children hear foul language from friends, older siblings, or parents at an early age. Just by walking down the street, they can encounter any number of colorful phrases, not to mention the obscene actions of people that they can witness. Children may revere someone who uses obscene language, but that person could just as easily be a parent or sibling and is not necessarily a musician. Eventually, everyone will be exposed to language they do not find acceptable. It is not solely the music artists' responsibility to restrict themselves for the sake of children. Censorship, in this case, is strongly biased and cannot *compensate* for the number of other places and people that a child could come across to encounter this type of language.

The question is: Who should decide what you read or view—the church, the government . . . or you? The answer to that question is *you*. Censorship on television channels such as Nickelodeon® or PBS® is understandable due to the fact that they mainly broadcast young children's programming. However, it is unnecessary to censor stations generally viewed (or listened to) by older audiences.

A few years ago, angry mothers and fathers sued artists and/or record companies for releasing albums that, without making note of the fact, contained explicit lyrics. They were concerned that their children might repeat these newly-learned words to teachers, principals, friends, and/or siblings. By law, record companies are now required to put stickers on cassette tapes and compact discs that say: "PARENTAL ADVISORY. EXPLICIT LYRICS."

Many parents also complained that the art on many album covers and within the contents of the albums themselves was too vulgar. For example, the Black Crowes' *Amorica* album, after its first release, was blasted by the media. The band chose to rerelease the album with the disputed sections of the cover blacked out completely.

If parents do not wish for their children to hear foul language, they should more closely supervise their children. While the government has taken an active role in this fight, it should not be expected to shoulder the full responsibility of limiting each child's access to adult themes and language. If a concerned parent is worried about her child's exposure to foul language and controversial music, it is not the artist's job to limit his creative freedom. The parent can always screen the album before allowing her child to hear it. If she doesn't like the content, she can always return it and decline her child's request to own it.

Many parents nowadays would rather have outside agencies limit their children than have to take on the responsibility themselves. Unfortunately, this attitude leads to the restriction—and sometimes the abolishment—of other people's freedoms. Under the First Amendment, we all have the right to express ourselves freely and openly. Censorship serves to kill that right and directly contradicts what it means to be an American.

1   Why did parents sue record companies and artists?

   A   The artists' lyrics may have caused children to use foul language.
   B   Record companies encouraged the use of foul lyrics on albums.
   C   The parents wanted album covers to be blacked out completely.
   D   Record companies labeled albums that contained foul content.

2   What is this article *mostly* about?

   A   How the government interprets the First Amendment
   B   Why the government should censor music more
   C   How censorship violates citizens' and artists' rights
   D   What parents should know about their kids' music

97

3 What is the function of the stickers record companies must put on some albums?

    A They let parents know which albums their children will like.
    B They allow artists to express their feelings about censorship.
    C They help parents choose suitable listening material for kids.
    D They inform listeners of the message conveyed in the music.

4 The author *most* likely wrote this article to—

    A analyze all the ways in which censorship can be harmful
    B instruct the readers on how their rights are being violated
    C persuade the reader to form an opinion against censorship
    D inform the reader of the correct way to raise their children

5 Why does the author think artists should be angry about censorship?

    A It limits their ability to express themselves.
    B Their album sales decrease in some places.
    C It does not allow them to use bad language.
    D They must make two versions of all songs.

6 What is the meaning of *compensate* as used in the article?

    A Argue
    B Pay
    C Make up for
    D Be forgiven

7 Why should parents supervise what their children listen to?

    A So they have something to talk about
    B Because the government does not do it
    C Because most artists are controversial
    D So they can decide what is appropriate

8 What is the meaning of *abridging* as used in the article?

    A Limiting
    B Crossing
    C Removing
    D Concerning

9 Based on the information in the article, do you think that censorship rules should apply equally to lyrics that are racist, lyrics that are violent, and lyrics that contain foul language? Why or why *not*? Based on his argument as presented in this article, what do you think the author of this article would say? Be sure to write your response in your answer document.

10 The author of this article has strong opinions on the role censorship plays in limiting people's freedoms. Do you think his argument is at all biased? Why or why *not*? Be sure to write your response in your answer document.

_____

_____

_____

_____

_____

_____

_____

_____

_____

_____

_____

_____

_____

_____

_____

_____

_____

_____

_____

_____

_____

_____

_____

from "THE FINANCIER"

by Theodore Dreiser

It was in his thirteenth year that young Cowperwood entered into his first business venture.

Walking along Front Street one day, a street of importing and wholesale establishments, he saw an auctioneer's flag hanging out before a wholesale grocery and from the interior came the auctioneer's voice: "What am I bid for this exceptional lot of Java coffee, twenty-two bags all told, which is now selling in the market for seven dollars and thirty-two cents a bag wholesale? What am I bid? What am I bid? The whole lot must go as one. What am I bid?"

"Eighteen dollars," suggested a trader standing near the door, more to start the bidding than anything else. Frank paused.

"Twenty-two!" called another.

"Thirty!" a third. "Thirty-five!" a fourth, and so up to seventy-five, less than half of what it was worth.

"I'm bid seventy-five! I'm bid seventy-five!" called the auctioneer, loudly. "Any other offers? Going once at seventy-five; am I offered eighty? Going twice at seventy-five, and"— he paused, one hand raised dramatically. Then he brought it down with a slap in the palm of the other—"sold to Mr. Silas Gregory for seventy-five. Make a note of that, Jerry," he called to his red-haired, freckle-faced clerk beside him. Then he turned to another lot of grocery staples—this time starch, eleven barrels of it.

Young Cowperwood was making a rapid calculation. If, as the auctioneer said, coffee was worth seven dollars and thirty-two cents a bag in the open market, and this buyer was getting this coffee for seventy-five dollars, he was making then and there eighty-six dollars and four cents, to say nothing of what his profit would be if he sold it at retail. As he recalled, his mother was paying twenty-eight cents a pound. He drew nearer, his books tucked under his arm, and watched these operations closely. The starch, as he soon heard, was valued at ten dollars a barrel, and it only brought six. Some kegs of vinegar were knocked down at one-third their value, and so on. He began to wish he could bid; but he had no money, just a little pocket change. The auctioneer noticed him standing almost directly under his nose, and was impressed with the stolidity—stolidity—of the boy's expression.

"I am going to offer you now a fine lot of Castile soap—seven cases, no less—which, as you know, if you know anything about soap, is now selling at fourteen cents a bar. This soap is worth anywhere at this moment eleven dollars and seventy-five cents a case. What am I bid? What am I bid? What am I bid?" He was talking fast in the usual style of auctioneers, with much unnecessary emphasis; but Cowperwood was not unduly impressed. He was already rapidly calculating for himself. Seven cases at eleven dollars and seventy-five cents would be worth just eighty-two dollars and twenty-five cents; and if it went at half—if it went at half—

"Twelve dollars," commented one bidder.

"Fifteen," bid another.

"Twenty," called a third.

"Twenty-five," a fourth.

Then it came to dollar raises, for Castile soap was not such a vital commodity.

"Twenty-six."

"Twenty-seven."

"Twenty-eight."

"Twenty-nine." There was a pause.

"Thirty," observed young Cowperwood, decisively.

The auctioneer, a short lean faced, spare man with bushy hair and an incisive eye, looked at him curiously and almost incredulously but without pausing. He had, somehow, in spite of himself, been impressed by the boy's peculiar eye. Now he felt, without knowing why, that the offer was probably legitimate enough, and that the boy had the money. He might be the son of a grocer.

"I'm bid thirty! I'm bid thirty! I'm bid thirty for this fine lot of Castile soap. It's a fine lot. It's worth fourteen cents a bar. Will any one bid thirty-one? Will any one bid thirty-one? Will any one bid thirty-one?"

"Thirty-one," said a voice.

"Thirty-two," replied Cowperwood. The same process was repeated.

"I'm bid thirty-two! I'm bid thirty-two! I'm bid thirty-two! Will anybody bid thirty-three? It's fine soap. Seven cases of fine Castile soap. Will anybody bid thirty-three?"

Young Cowperwood's mind was working. He had no money with him; but his father was teller of the Third National Bank, and he could quote him as reference. He could sell all of his soap to the family grocer, surely; or, if not, to other grocers. Other people were anxious to get this soap at this price. Why not he?

The auctioneer paused.

"Thirty-two once! Am I bid thirty-three? Thirty-two twice! Am I bid thirty-three? Thirty-two three times! Seven fine cases of soap. Am I bid anything more? Once, twice! Three times! Am I bid anything more?"—his hand was up again—"and sold to Mr.—?" He leaned over and looked curiously into the face of his young bidder.

"Frank Cowperwood, son of the teller of the Third National Bank," replied the boy, decisively.

"Oh, yes," said the man, fixed by his glance.

"Will you wait while I run up to the bank and get the money?"

"Yes. Don't be gone long. If you're not here in an hour I'll sell it again."

Young Cowperwood made no reply. He hurried out and ran fast; first, to his mother's grocer, whose store was within a block of his home.

Thirty feet from the door he slowed up, put on a nonchalant air, and strolling in, looked about for Castile soap. There it was, the same kind, displayed in a box and looking just as his soap looked.

"How much is this a bar, Mr. Dalrymple?" he inquired.

"Sixteen cents," replied that worthy.

"If I could sell you seven boxes for sixty-two dollars just like this, would you take them?"

"The same soap?"

"Yes, sir."

Mr. Dalrymple calculated a moment.

"Yes, I think I would," he replied, cautiously.

"Would you pay me to-day?"

"I'd give you my note for it. Where is the soap?"

He was perplexed and somewhat astonished by this unexpected proposition on the part of his neighbor's son. He knew Mr. Cowperwood well—and Frank also.

"Will you take it if I bring it to you to-day?"

"Yes, I will," he replied. "Are you going into the soap business?"

"No. But I know where I can get some of that soap cheap."

104

He hurried out again and ran to his father's bank. It was after banking hours; but he knew how to get in, and he knew that his father would be glad to see him make thirty dollars. He only wanted to borrow the money for a day.

"What's the trouble, Frank?" asked his father, looking up from his desk when he appeared, breathless and red faced.

"I want you to loan me thirty-two dollars! Will you?"

"Why, yes, I might. What do you want to do with it?"

"I want to buy some soap—seven bars of Castile soap. I know where I can get it and sell it. Mr. Dalrymple will take it. He's already offered me sixty-two for it. I can get it for thirty-two. Will you let me have the money? I've got to run back and pay the auctioneer."

His father smiled. This was the most business-like attitude he had seen his son manifest.

He was so keen, so alert for a boy of thirteen.

"Why, Frank," he said, going over to a drawer where some bills were, "are you going to become a financier already? You're sure you're not going to lose on this? You know what you're doing, do you?"

"You let me have the money, father, will you?" he pleaded. "I'll show you in a little bit. Just let me have it. You can trust me."

He was like a young hound on the scent of game. His father could not resist his appeal.

"Why, certainly, Frank," he replied. "I'll trust you." And he counted out six five-dollar certificates of the Third National's own issue and two ones. "There you are."

Frank ran out of the building with a briefly spoken thanks and returned to the auction room as fast as his legs would carry him. When he came in, sugar was being auctioned. He made his way to the auctioneer's clerk.

"I want to pay for that soap," he suggested.

"Now?"

"Yes. Will you give me a receipt?"

"Yep."

"Do you deliver this?"

"No. No delivery. You have to take it away in twenty-four hours."

That difficulty did not trouble him.

"All right," he said, and pocketed his paper testimony of purchase.

The auctioneer watched him as he went out. In half an hour he was back with a drayman—an idle levee-wharf hanger-on who was waiting for a job.

Frank had bargained with him to deliver the soap for sixty cents. In still another half-hour he was before the door of the astonished Mr. Dalrymple whom he had come out and look at the boxes before attempting to remove them. His plan was to have them carried on to his own home if the operation for any reason failed to go through. Though it was his first great venture, he was cool as glass.

"Yes," said Mr. Dalrymple, scratching his gray head reflectively. "Yes, that's the same soap. I'll take it. I'll be as good as my word. Where'd you get it, Frank?"

"At Bixom's auction up here," he replied, frankly and blandly.

Mr. Dalrymple had the drayman bring in the soap; and after some formality— because the agent in this case was a boy—made out his note at thirty days and gave it to him.

Frank thanked him and pocketed the note. He decided to go back to his father's bank and discount it, as he had seen others doing, thereby paying his father back and getting his own profit in ready money. It couldn't be done ordinarily on any day after business hours; but his father would make an exception in his case.

He hurried back, whistling; and his father glanced up smiling when he came in.

"Well, Frank, how'd you make out?" he asked.

"Here's a note at thirty days," he said, producing the paper Dalrymple had given him. "Do you want to discount that for me? You can take your thirty-two out of that."

His father examined it closely. "Sixty-two dollars!" he observed. "Mr. Dalrymple! That's good paper! Yes, I can. It will cost you ten per cent," he added, jestingly. "Why don't you just hold it, though? I'll let you have the thirty-two dollars until the end of the month."

"Oh, no," said his son, "you discount it and take your money. I may want mine."

His father smiled at his business-like air. "All right," he said. "I'll fix it to-morrow. Tell me just how you did this." And his son told him.

At seven o'clock that evening Frank's mother heard about it, and in due time Uncle Seneca.

"What'd I tell you, Cowperwood?" he asked. "He has stuff in him, that youngster. Look out for him."

106

Mrs. Cowperwood looked at her boy curiously at dinner. Was this the son she had nursed at her bosom not so very long before? Surely he was developing rapidly.

"Well, Frank, I hope you can do that often," she said.

"I hope so, too, ma," was his rather noncommittal reply.

Auction sales were not to be discovered every day, however, and his home grocer was only open to one such transaction in a reasonable period of time, but from the very first young Cowperwood knew how to make money. He took subscriptions for a boys' paper, handled the agency for the sale of a new kind of ice-skate, and once organized a band of neighborhood youths into a union for the purpose of purchasing their summer straw hats at wholesale. It was not his idea that he could get rich by saving. From the first he had the notion that liberal spending was better, and that somehow he would get along.

It was in this year, or a little earlier, that he began to take an interest in girls. He had from the first a keen eye for the beautiful among them; and, being good-looking and magnetic himself, it was not difficult for him to attract the sympathetic interest of those in whom he was interested. A twelve-year-old girl, Patience Barlow, who lived further up the street, was the first to attract his attention or be attracted by him. Black hair and snapping black eyes were her portion, with pretty pigtails down her back, and dainty feet and ankles to match a dainty figure. She was a Quakeress, the daughter of Quaker parents, wearing a demure little bonnet. Her disposition, however, was *vivacious*, and she liked this self-reliant, self-sufficient, straight-spoken boy. One day, after an exchange of glances from time to time, he said, with a smile and the courage that was innate to him: "You live up my way, don't you?"

"Yes," she replied, a little flustered—this last manifested in a nervous swinging of her school-bag—"I live at number one-forty-one."

"I know the house," he said. "I've seen you go in there. You go to the same school my sister does, don't you? Aren't you Patience Barlow?" He had heard some of the boys speak her name.

"Yes. How do you know?"

"Oh, I've heard," he smiled. "I've seen you. Do you like licorice?"

He fished in his coat and pulled out some fresh sticks that were sold at the time.

"Thank you," she said, sweetly, taking one.

"It isn't very good. I've been carrying it a long time. I had some taffy the other day."

"Oh, it's all right," she replied, chewing the end of hers.

"Don't you know my sister, Anna Cowperwood?" he recurred, by way of self-introduction.

"She's in a lower grade than you are, but I thought maybe you might have seen her."

"I think I know who she is. I've seen her coming home from school."

"I live right over there," he confided, pointing to his own home as he drew near to it, as if she didn't know. "I'll see you around here now, I guess."

"Do you know Ruth Merriam?" she asked, when he was about ready to turn off into the cobblestone road to reach his own door.

"No, why?"

"She's giving a party next Tuesday," she volunteered, seemingly pointlessly, but only seemingly.

"Where does she live?"

"There in twenty-eight."

"I'd like to go," he affirmed, warmly, as he swung away from her.

"Maybe she'll ask you," she called back, growing more courageous as the distance between them widened. "I'll ask her."

"Thanks," he smiled.

And she began to run gaily onward.

He looked after her with a smiling face. She was very pretty. He felt a keen desire to kiss her, and what might transpire at Ruth Merriam's party rose vividly before his eyes.

This was just one of the early love affairs, or puppy loves, that held his mind from time to time in the mixture of after events. Patience Barlow was kissed by him in secret ways many times before he found another girl. She and others of the street ran out to play in the snow of a winter's night, or lingered after dusk before her own door when the days grew dark early. It was so easy to catch and kiss her then, and to talk to her foolishly at parties.

Then came Dora Fitler, when he was sixteen years old and she was fourteen; and Marjorie Stafford, when he was seventeen and she was fifteen. Dora Fitler was a brunette, and Marjorie Stafford was as fair as the morning, with bright-red cheeks, bluish-gray eyes, and flaxen hair, and as plump as a partridge.

108

1   Which word *best* describes Frank Cowperwood's father's reaction to Frank's request for money?

   A   Shocked
   B   Doubtful
   C   Unfair
   D   Proud

2   Why can't Frank buy and sell groceries every day?

   A   He does not have the money to buy anything else.
   B   He cannot sell things to Mr. Dalrymple daily.
   C   He never has the time because of the boys' union.
   D   He would rather play with children his own age.

3   What is the meaning of *vivacious* as used in the story?

   A   Vicious
   B   Lively
   C   Reserved
   D   Greedy

4   Which word *best* describes Frank's attitude?

   A   Confident
   B   Hesitant
   C   Foolish
   D   Unreliable

5 What does ". . . he was cool as glass" mean as used in the story?

    A He was not fooling anyone.
    B He was deceiving someone.
    C He was calm and relaxed.
    D He was cunning and sly.

6 What does the Castile soap *most* likely symbolize?

    A Romance
    B Ambition
    C Dishonesty
    D Cleanliness

7 Which of these will *most* likely happen next?

    A Mr. Dalrymple will only buy from Frank
    B Frank will grow up to be successful.
    C The auctioneer will be mad at Frank.
    D Frank will marry Marjorie one day.

8 Why is Frank making rapid calculations in his head?

    A He wonders if his father will approve of the high price.
    B He is not sure he has enough money to pay for the soap.
    C He is figuring out how much the auctioneer is making.
    D He wants to know if he can make money on the soap.

9 Which of these *best* describes a theme of the story?

    A Hasty purchases result in wasted money.

    B A business-like mind can lead to wealth.

    C Young love is a dangerous distraction.

    D It is unwise to take candy from strangers.

10 Identify and explain how Frank could have lost money on the deal he made with Mr. Dalrymple. Be sure to write your response in your answer document.

11 Describe a skill that you have learned to do well. Compare how you learned and have used this skill with Frank's experiences. Use details from the story to support your answer. Be sure to write your response in your answer document.

_____

_____

_____

_____

_____

_____

_____

_____

_____

_____

_____

_____

_____

_____

_____

_____

_____

_____

_____

_____

_____

_____

_____

_____

POISON IVY AND ITS COUSINS

The poison ivy plant is the *bane* of millions of campers, hikers, gardeners, and others who enjoy the great outdoors. So are its cousins: poison oak and poison sumac. Approximately 85 percent of the population will develop an allergic reaction if exposed to poison ivy, oak, or sumac. Usually, people develop a sensitivity to poison ivy, oak, or sumac only after several encounters with the plants. However, sensitivity may occur after only one exposure.

The cause of the rash, blisters, and infamous itch is "urushiol." It is a chemical in the sap of poison ivy, oak, and sumac plants. Because urushiol is inside the plant, brushing against an intact plant will not cause a reaction. But undamaged plants are rare. Stems or leaves broken by the wind or by animals and even the tiny holes made by chewing insects can release urushiol.

Reactions, treatments and preventive measures are the same for all three poison plants. Avoiding direct contact with the plants reduces the risk, but doesn't guarantee against a reaction. Urushiol can stick to pets, garden tools, balls, or anything it comes in contact with. If the urushiol isn't washed off those objects or animals, just touching them could cause a reaction in a susceptible person.

Urushiol that's rubbed off the plants onto other things can remain potent for years, depending on the environment. If the contaminated object is in a dry environment, the potency of the urushiol can last for decades. Even if the environment is warm and moist, the urushiol could still cause a reaction a year later.

Almost all parts of the body are vulnerable to the sticky urushiol. Because the chemical must penetrate the skin to cause a reaction, places where the skin is thick, such as the soles of the feet and the palms of the hands, are less sensitive to the sap than areas where the skin is thinner. The severity of the reaction may also depend on how large a dose of urushiol the person gets.

Urushiol can penetrate the skin within minutes. There is no time to waste if you know that you have been exposed. The earlier you cleanse the skin, the greater the chance that you can remove the urushiol before it gets through the skin. Cleansing may not stop the initial rash if more than ten minutes has elapsed. However, it can help prevent the rash from spreading further.

If you've been exposed to poison ivy, oak, or sumac, stay indoors until you complete the first two steps: Cleanse exposed skin with generous amounts of rubbing alcohol. Don't go near plants the same day. Alcohol removes your skin's protection as well as the urushiol. Any new contact will cause the urushiol to penetrate twice as fast.

113

1   The reader can conclude that poison ivy, poison oak, and poison sumac all—

   A   have reactions that are very different
   B   have leaves that look similar
   C   contain very different chemicals
   D   have the same treatment

2   What is the meaning of *bane* as used in the article?

   A   Bother
   B   Fear
   C   Break
   D   Hinder

3   When does urushiol last the longest?

   A   In a very hot environment
   B   In a warm and moist environment
   C   In a very dry environment
   D   In a cool and moist environment

114

4 Why is cleaning with alcohol both helpful and dangerous? Use at least one detail from the article to support your answer. Be sure to write your response in your answer document.

_____

_____

_____

_____

_____

_____

_____

_____

_____

_____

_____

_____

_____

_____

_____

_____

_____

_____

_____

_____

_____

_____

_____

JAMES P. BECKWOURTH, BLACK MOUNTAIN MAN

Trapping beaver and other animals for their fur in the early 1800s was a lonely and often dangerous way of life. Living under difficult conditions and forced to hunt daily for food, it was not a profession undertaken lightly. The privations were made up for with the chance to become rich in a short period of time. What few know, however, is that the fur trade empires created opportunities for people from many ethnic backgrounds. Trappers included Hawaiians, native New Mexicans, French Canadians, people of African ancestry, and eastern American Indians from the Shawnee, Delaware, and Iroquois tribes.

Of the black trappers making a living in the Rocky Mountains, none is as well known as James P. Beckwourth. He was born to Jennings Beckwith, a slaveowner, and a plantation slave named Miss Kill in Frederick County, Virginia around 1797.

One of several mixed-race siblings, young James Beckwith moved with his father to St. Louis, Missouri, in the early years of the nineteenth century. As a boy, he learned about his natural surroundings. He spent time hunting in the outskirts of French St. Louis. He apprenticed to a blacksmith. After a while, he ran away. Later, he became part of a trapping expedition on the Wood River.

Drawn to the outdoor life, Beckwith changed his name to Beckwourth. He joined the 1825 trapping party to the Rocky Mountains led by General William H. Ashley. The black mountain man claimed to have lived with the Blackfoot and later the Crow peoples. He learned the Crow language and married several Crow women. In 1825, Ashley made himself rich by reintroducing an American Indian idea. He brought goods and supplies to a prearranged place in the mountains. There he traded his goods for the trappers' pelts.

As a trapper for Ashley, Beckwourth rubbed shoulders with many of the famous trappers of his day. He was a *contemporary* of such men as Jim Bridger, Christopher "Kit" Carson, Tom "Broken Hand" Fitzpatrick, and Moses "Black" Harris. Beckwourth claimed to have been part of a group of trappers who established El Pueblo, a trading post on the Arkansas River that later became the city of Pueblo, Colorado.

Beckwourth found a freedom in the mountains that would not have been possible for a black man anywhere else in the United States at that time. Beckwourth worked as an independent trader and as an employee of Bent, St. Vrain and Co. at Bent's Old Fort and for the American Fur Company.

Beckwourth traveled to New Mexico where he opened a hotel and gambling parlor. From there he took dispatches to California for the U.S. military. He later moved to California during the "Gold Rush." There he set up a store. He also discovered a pass in the Sierra Nevada Mountains that is still called "Beckwourth Pass."

Beckwourth followed gold miners to Colorado in 1859. He was a part of the beginnings of Denver, Colorado. Always restless, Beckwourth traveled back and forth across the west until taking a job as an interpreter for the 1866 Carrington Expedition out of Fort Laramie, Wyoming.

Riding to Fort C.F. Smith in what is Montana today, Beckwourth complained of headaches and nosebleeds. He stopped in the camp of his old friends, the Crow. There Beckwourth suffered symptoms of a stroke. He died at sixty-seven or sixty-eight years of age. He was buried on Crow land in that same area near the present Bighorn Canyon National Recreation Area. James Beckwourth's final resting place was far from his Virginia birthplace, but fitting for this African-American adventurer.

1   The author *most* likely includes the first paragraph to—

   A   analyze the desire for fur
   B   describe trappers' lives
   C   introduce Beckwourth
   D   connect the present to the past

2   Which word *best* describes the tone of this article?

   A   Delicate
   B   Uncertain
   C   Instructive
   D   Amusing

3   Beckwourth *first* learned to love the outdoors by—

   A   living among the Crow people
   B   being raised by Miss Kill
   C   hunting in St. Louis
   D   meeting "Kit" Carson

4   What is the meaning of *contemporary* as used in the article?

    A   Peer

    B   Seller

    C   Hunter

    D   Finder

5   Why do you think Beckwourth probably chose to live and die among the Crow? Be sure to write your response in your answer document.

AFRICAN AMERICANS IN COMBAT

"We officers of the Tenth Cavalry could have taken our black heroes into our arms. They had fought their way into our affections, as they have fought their way into the hearts of the American people." General John J. Pershing wrote these words. He was referring to the all-black 10th U.S. Cavalry that he had commanded during the battle of San Juan Hill, July 1, 1898.

General Pershing wrote the following words as well. They were part of a secret communiqué addressed to the French military stationed with the American army. It was dated August 7, 1918.

We must prevent the rise of any pronounced degree of intimacy between French officers and Black officers. We may be courteous and amiable with the last but we cannot deal with them on the same plane as white American officers without deeply wounding the latter. We must not eat with them, must not shake hands with them, seek to talk to them or to meet with them outside the requirements of military service. We must not commend too highly these troops, especially in front of white Americans. Make a point of keeping the native cantonment from spoiling the Negro. White Americans become very incensed at any particular expression of intimacy between white women and black men.

Five months after General Pershing praised black fighting men at San Juan Hill, that same regiment was stationed in Huntsville, Alabama. There, a black civilian killed two black enlisted men. He had been apparently motivated by a belief that whites would pay a reward for every dead black soldier. This is an example of the confusion regarding the worth of the black soldier and sailor in American military service.

Blacks contributed to the defense of the colonies long before the American Revolution, but were excluded from the colonial militia in peacetime. In fact, there has been no U.S. war and few battles that have not involved Americans of African descent. They fought on both sides in the American Revolution. They have been in every war, declared or otherwise, from that time until the present.

Until 1948, the American military had always been segregated. In peacetime, the country—and the southern states in particular—were reluctant to arm blacks. And in war, the country generally allowed blacks to serve only after white recruitment shortages became an issue. In spite of that, African Americans often served honorably and fought hard overseas to win or preserve freedoms that they themselves did not enjoy at home.

The story of African Americans in combat is little different from the story of whites in the military. There have been heroes and there have been cowards. There has been competence and there has been ineptitude. However, there are two exceptions. There are two things that make the experience different. The first exception is that blacks have always had to deal with racism while proving that the stereotype of the unfit black warrior is false.

The second exception is that the black warriors have often been invisible to the public. Television and movies, from which so many Americans learn about history, have often *glorified* white heroes. Many shows have not even mentioned the roles played by black soldiers and sailors. In the popular 1970 movie, *Patton*, the main character is played by George C. Scott; General George S. Patton, Jr., gives a famous and memorable speech to a battalion of white soldiers. In fact, that famous speech was actually given to the all-black 761st Tank Battalion.

1 What is the meaning of *glorified* as used in the article?

   A Offended
   B Praised
   C Requested
   D Attracted

2 The author *most* likely wrote this article to—

   A tell readers about the adventures of an African American soldier
   B encourage readers to show their support for soldiers in the military
   C explain how French soldiers and African American soldiers got along
   D show how African American soldiers were often treated unfairly

3 Which word *best* describes how General Pershing is portrayed?

   A Dishonest
   B Humorous
   C Supportive
   D Observant

from "THE RED-HEADED LEAGUE"

by Arthur Conan Doyle

There was nothing in the office but a couple of wooden chairs and a deal table, behind which sat a small man, with a head that was even redder than mine. He said a few words to each candidate as he came up, and then he always managed to find some fault in them which would disqualify them. Getting a vacancy did not seem to be such a very easy matter after all. However, when our turn came, the little man was much more favorable to me than to any of the others, and he closed the door as we entered, so that he might have a private word with us.

"This is Mr. Jabez Wilson," said my assistant, "and he is willing to fill a vacancy in the League."

"And he is admirably suited for it," the other answered. "He has every requirement. I cannot recall when I have seen anything so fine." He took a step backward, cocked his head on one side, and gazed at my hair until I felt quite bashful. Then suddenly he plunged forward, wrung my hand, and congratulated me warmly on my success.

"It would be injustice to hesitate," said he. "You will, however, I am sure, excuse me for taking an obvious precaution." With that he seized my hair in both his hands, and tugged until I yelled with the pain. "There is water in your eyes," said he, as he released me. "I *perceive* that all is as it should be. But we have to be careful, for we have twice been deceived by wigs and once by paint. I could tell you tales of cobbler's wax which would disgust you with human nature." He stepped over to the window and shouted through it at the top of his voice that the vacancy was filled. A groan of disappointment came up from below, and the folk all trooped away in different directions, until there was not a red head to be seen except my own and that of the manager.

"My name," said he, "is Mr. Duncan Ross, and I am myself one of the pensioners upon the fund left by our noble benefactor. Are you a married man, Mr. Wilson? Have you a family?"

I answered that I had not.

His face fell immediately.

"Dear me!" he said, gravely, "that is very serious indeed! I am sorry to hear you say that. The fund was, of course, for the propagation and spread of the red heads as well as for their maintenance. It is exceedingly unfortunate that you should be a bachelor."

My face lengthened at this, Mr. Holmes, for I thought that I was not to have the vacancy after all; but, after thinking it over for a few minutes, he said that it would be all right.

"In the case of another," said he, "the objection might be fatal, but we must stretch a point in favor of a man with such a head of hair as yours. When shall you be able to enter upon your new duties?"

121

"Well, it is a little awkward, for I have a business already," said I.

"Oh, never mind about that, Mr. Wilson!" said Vincent Spaulding. "I shall be able to look after that for you."

"What would be the hours?" I asked.

"Ten to two."

Now a pawnbroker's business is mostly done of an evening, Mr. Holmes, especially Thursday and Friday evenings, which is just before pay day; so it would suit me very well to earn a little in the mornings. Besides, I knew that my assistant was a good man, and that he would see to anything that turned up.

"That would suit me very well," said I. "And the pay?"

"Is four pounds a week."

"And the work?"

"Is purely nominal."

"What do you call purely nominal?"

"Well, you have to be in the office, or at least in the building, the whole time. If you leave, you forfeit your whole position forever. The will is very clear upon that point. You don't comply with the conditions if you budge from the office during that time."

"It's only four hours a day, and I should not think of leaving," said I.

"No excuse will avail," said Mr. Duncan Ross, "neither sickness, nor business, nor anything else. There you must stay, or you lose your billet."

"And the work?"

"Is to copy out the 'Encyclopaedia Britannica.' There is the first volume of it in that press. You must find your own ink, pens, and blotting paper, but we provide this table and chair. Will you be ready tomorrow?'

"Certainly," I answered.

"Then, good-by, Mr. Jabez Wilson, and let me congratulate you once more on the important position which you have been fortunate enough to gain." He bowed me out of the room, and I went home with my assistant hardly knowing what to say or do, I was so pleased at my own good fortune.

122

1 Jabez Wilson was considered perfect for the job because—

  A he did not have children
  B he was friends with Duncan Ross
  C he had fine red hair
  D he spoke with Mr. Holmes

2 Wilson feared that he would be rejected when—

  A he saw other red heads outside
  B Ross closely examined his hair
  C Spaulding offered to run his business
  D he admitted he was not married

3 What is the meaning of *perceive* as used in the story?

  A Recognize
  B Follow
  C Criticize
  D Tolerate

4 Which word *best* describes how the narrator feels at the end of the story?

  A Peaceful
  B Satisfied
  C Unhappy
  D Nervous

5 What do you think the purpose of the Red-Headed League might have been? Be sure to write your response in your answer document.

_____

_____

_____

_____

_____

_____

_____

_____

_____

_____

_____

_____

_____

_____

_____

_____

_____

_____

_____

_____

_____

_____

THE QUEST FOR HAPPINESS

from "DELICATESSEN"
by Joyce Kilmer

Here is a shop of wonderment.
From every land has come a prize;
Rich spices from the Orient,
And fruit that knew Italian skies,

And figs that ripened by the sea
In Smyrna, nuts from hot Brazil,
Strange pungent meats from
    Germany,
And currants from a Grecian hill.

He is the lord of goodly things
That make the poor man's table gay,
Yet of his worth no minstrel sings
And on his tomb there is no bay.

Perhaps he lives and dies unpraised,
This trafficker in humble sweets,
Because his little shops are raised
By thousands in the city streets.

Yet stars in greater numbers shine,
And violets in millions grow,
And they in many a golden line
Are sung, as every child must know.
Perhaps Fame thinks his worried
    eyes,
His wrinkled, shrewd, pathetic face,
His shop, and all he sells and buys,
Are desperately commonplace.

Well, it is true he has no sword
To dangle at his booted knees.
He leans across a slab of board,
And draws his knife and slices cheese.

He never heard of chivalry,
He longs for no heroic times;
He thinks of pickles, olives, tea,
And dollars, nickels, cents and dimes.

His world has narrow walls, it seems;
By counters is his soul confined;
His wares are all his hopes and
    dreams,
They are the fabric of his mind.

Yet—in a room above the store
There is a woman—and a child
Pattered just now across the floor;
The shopman looked at him and
    smiled.

For, once he thrilled with high
    romance
And tuned to love his eager voice.
Like any cavalier of France
He wooed the maiden of his choice.

And now deep in his weary heart
Are sacred flames that whitely burn.
He has of Heaven's grace a part
Who loves, who is beloved in turn.

And when the long day's work is done,
(How slow the leaden minutes ran!)
Home, with his wife and little son,
He is no huckster, but a man!

He decks his window artfully,
He haggles over paltry sums.
In this strange field his war must be
And by such blows his triumph comes.

What if no trumpet sounds to call
His armed legions to his side?
What if, to no ancestral hall
He comes in all a victor's pride?

This man has home and child and
    wife
And battle set for every day.
This man has God and love and life;
These stand, all else shall pass away.

"YOUNG LOCHINVAR"
by Sir Walter Scott

Oh young Lochinvar is come out of the west,
Through all the wide Border his steed was the best;
And save his good broadsword he weapon had none;
He rode all unarm'd, and he rode all alone.
So faithful in love, and so dauntless in war,
There never was knight like the young Lochinvar.

He staid not for brake, and he stopp'd not for stone,
He swam the Esk river where ford there was none;
But ere he alighted at Netherby gate,
The bride had consented, the gallant came late:
For a laggard in love, and a dastard in war,
Was to wed the fair Ellen of brave Lochinvar.

So boldly he enter'd the Netherby Hall,
Among brid'smen, and kinsmen, and brothers, and all;
Then spoke the bride's father, his hand on his sword,
(For the poor craven bridegroom said never a word,)
"O come ye in peace here, or come ye in war,
Or to dance at our bridal, young Lord Lochinvar?"—

"I long woo'd your daughter, my suit you denied;—
Love swells like the Solway, but ebbs like its tide—
And now am I come, with this lost love of mine,
To lead but one measure, drink one cup of wine.
There are maidens in Scotland more lovely by far,
That would gladly be bride to the young Lochinvar."

The bride kiss'd the goblet; the knight took it up,
He quaff'd off the wine, and he threw down the cup.
She look'd down to blush, and she look'd up to sigh,
With a smile on her lips, and a tear in her eye.
He took her soft hand, ere her mother could bar,—
"Now tread we a measure!" said young Lochinvar.

So stately his form, and so lovely her face,
That never a hall such a galliard did grace;
While her mother did fret, and her father did fume,
And the bridegroom stood dangling his bonnet and plume;
And the bride-maidens whispered, " 'T were better by far,
To have match'd our fair cousin with young Lochinvar."

One touch to her hand, and one word in her ear,
When they reach'd the hall-door, and the charger stood near;
So light to the croupe the fair lady he swung,
So light to the saddle before her he sprung!

126

"She is won! we are gone, over bank, bush, and scaur;
They'll have fleet steeds that follow," quoth young Lochinvar.

There was mounting 'mong Græmes of the Netherby clan;
Forsters, Fenwicks, and Musgraves, they rode and they ran:
There was racing and chasing on Cannobie Lea,
But the lost bride of Netherby ne'er did they see.
So daring in love, and so dauntless in war,
Have ye e'er heard of gallant like young Lochinvar?

1   Which word *best* describes the tone in the first poem?

   A   Tense
   B   Joyful
   C   Serious
   D   Angry

2   Which word *best* describes what the shopkeeper fights for?

   A   Survival
   B   Fame
   C   Glory
   D   Riches

3   What does the shopkeeper think is *most* important?

   A   His store
   B   Adventure
   C   His family
   D   Romance

4 Which word *best* describes the bridegroom from the second poem?

   A Brave

   B Gallant

   C Cowardly

   D Lovely

5 What did young Lochinvar tell Ellen's father?

   A He was in love with Ellen.

   B He had come to woo Ellen.

   C He thought Ellen was pretty.

   D He didn't want to fight him.

6 At the wedding, Lochinvar and Ellen—

   A danced together

   B held hands

   C drank together

   D ignored each other

7 How do the bridesmaids feel about Lochinvar?

   A He is very rude to their fair cousin.

   B He is better suited to their cousin.

   C He is too lazy to be with their cousin.

   D He is cruel and violent to their cousin.

8 What characteristic do these two poems share?

   A They concern a spirited adventure with many characters.

   B They concern a character's illness and slow recovery.

   C They focus on character's battle for what they want.

   D They focus on a humorous story about far away places.

9 Why does the first poet think that a delicatessen owner is worth writing about? Do you agree? Be sure to write your response in your answer document.

_____

_____

_____

_____

_____

_____

_____

_____

_____

_____

_____

_____

_____

_____

_____

_____

_____

_____

_____

_____

_____

_____

_____

_____

10 Why do you think Lochinvar waited so long before stealing Ellen away? Be sure to write your response in your answer document.

_____

_____

_____

_____

_____

_____

_____

_____

_____

_____

_____

_____

_____

_____

_____

_____

_____

_____

_____

_____

_____

_____

"GET UP AND BAR THE DOOR"

I.

IT fell about the Martinmas time,
And a gay time it was then,
When our goodwife got puddings to
    make,
And she's boil'd them in the pan.

II.

The wind sae cauld blew south and
    north,
And blew into the floor;
Quoth our goodman to our goodwife,
'Gae out and bar the door.'—

III.

'My hand is in my hussyfskap,
Goodman, as ye may see;
An' it shou'dna be barr'd this
    hundred year,
It's no be barr'd for me.'—

IV.

They made a paction 'tween them
    twa,
They made it firm and sure,
That the first word whae'er shou'd
    speak,
Shou'd rise and bar the door.

V.

Then by there came two gentlemen,
At twelve o' clock at night,
And they could neither see house
    nor hall,
Nor coal nor candle-light.

VI.

Now whether is this a rich man's
    house,
Or whether is it a poor?'
But ne'er a word wad ane o' them
    speak,
For barring of the door.

VII.

And first they ate the white
    puddings,
And then they ate the black.
Tho' muckle thought the goodwife to
    hersel'
Yet ne'er a word she spake.

VIII.

Then said the one unto the other,
'Here, man, tak ye my knife;
Do ye tak aff the auld man's beard,
And I'll kiss the goodwife.'—

IX.

'But there's nae water in the house,
And what shall we do than?'—
'What ails ye at the pudding-broo,
That boils into the pan?'

X.

O up then started our goodman,
An angry man was he:
'Will ye kiss my wife before my een,
And sca'd me wi' pudding-bree?'

XI.

Then up and started our goodwife,
Gied three skips on the floor:
'Goodman, you've spoken the
    foremost word!
Get up and bar the door.'

1 Which of these *best* describes what this poem is about?

    A Two foolish robbers
    B Two stubborn people
    C People and nature
    D Money and power

2 The man told his wife to close the door because—

    A a cold wind was blowing in
    B it would soon be midnight
    C bugs were getting in the house
    D the snow began to come inside

3 The wife couldn't close the door because—

    A the storm was too strong to close it
    B the snow was blocking the doorway
    C they had visitors coming to the house
    D she was too busy making pudding

4 The man *most* likely speaks up because—

    A the visitors eat his pudding
    B his wife is going to leave
    C he doesn't want to be burned
    D he wants the door closed

5 Which word *best* describes the men who came at midnight?

    A Soldiers
    B Neighbors
    C Robbers
    D Students

6 Which word *best* describes the husband and wife's situation?

A Humorous
B Cautious
C Pleasant
D Dangerous

7 Which word *best* describes how the husband feels when the two men come in?

A Angry
B Nervous
C Excited
D Disappointed

8 What happens after the men come in?

A The husband bars the door.
B The husband eats the pudding.
C The visitors bar the door.
D The visitors eat the pudding.

9 Read the following stanza from the poem and then answer the question.

"The wind sae cauld blew south and north,

And blew into the floor;

Quoth our goodman to our goodwife,

'Gae out and bar the door.'"

The author probably chooses to call the woman "our" goodwife to show that—

A the man is married to her
B the man likes her pudding
C she is the poem's subject
D she won by not speaking

10 Think about the husband and wife from the poem. Write a story or poem about two other stubborn people. Be sure to write your response in your answer document.

_____

_____

_____

_____

_____

_____

_____

_____

_____

_____

_____

_____

_____

_____

_____

_____

_____

_____

_____

_____

_____

_____

_____

_____

134

Robert Service was born in Preston, Lancashire, England. His parents were Scottish. He spent his childhood in Scotland. He attended the University of Glasgow. His vagabond career took him throughout the world. He worked at a wide variety of jobs, from cook to clerk, from hobo to correspondent. He emigrated to Canada in 1894. He took a job with the Canadian Bank of Commerce. He was stationed for eight years in Whitehorse, Yukon. It was while in the Yukon that he published his first book of poems, *Songs of a Sourdough*. It was to make him famous.

Writing became a career. He was a correspondent for *The Toronto Star* during the Balkan Wars of 1912–1913. He was an ambulance driver and correspondent in France during World War I. He settled in France after World War I and married a French woman.

"THE MEN THAT DON' T FIT IN"
by Robert W. Service

There's a race of men that don't fit in,
A race that can't stay still;
So they break the hearts of kith and kin,
And they roam the world at will.
They range the field and they rove the flood,
And they climb the mountain's crest;
Theirs is the curse of the gypsy blood,
And they don't know how to rest.

If they just went straight they might go far;
They are strong and brave and true;
But they're always tired of the things that are,
And they want the strange and new.
They say: "Could I find my proper groove,
What a deep mark I would make!"
So they chop and change, and each fresh move
Is only a fresh mistake.

And each forgets, as he strips and runs
With a brilliant, fitful pace,
It's the steady, quiet, plodding ones
Who win in the lifelong *race*.
And each forgets that his youth has fled,
Forgets that his prime is past,
Till he stands one day, with a hope that's dead,
In the glare of the truth at last.

He has failed, he has failed; he has missed his chance;
He has just done things by half.
Life's been a jolly good joke on him,
And now is the time to laugh.
Ha, ha! He is one of the Legion Lost;
He was never meant to win;
He's a rolling stone, and it's bred in the bone;
He's a man who won't fit in.

1   Which word *best* describes "men that don't fit in" as the get older?

   A   Silly
   B   Tired
   C   Regretful
   D   Satisfied

2   Read the following stanza from the poem and then answer the question.

"They range the field and they rove the flood,

And they climb the mountain's crest;

Theirs is the curse of the gypsy blood,

And they don't know how to rest."

The author probably chooses to write "They range the field and they rove the flood" to show that the men—

   A   go hunting for food
   B   are often restless
   C   try to help people
   D   hope to find homes

3 What is the meaning of *race* as used in the poem?

   A Run
   B Group
   C Time
   D Contest

4 Think about how the poet describes the men in the poem. Which do you think the poet thinks is best: a steady, quiet, plodding life, or a wild, wandering adventurous life? Why? Be sure to write your response in your answer document.

137

Harriet Beecher Stowe was born June 14, 1811, in Litchfield, Connecticut. Her father, the Reverend Lyman Beecher (1775-1863), was a prominent Congregational minister. Harriet was a student at Hartford Female Seminary. The school had been founded by her sister, Catharine. Harriet later taught there.

In 1832, Harriet moved with her family to Cincinnati, Ohio. Her father became president of Lane Theological Seminary. In Cincinnati, Harriet married Calvin E. Stowe. He was a professor at Lane. Cincinnati was just across the river from Kentucky. Kentucky was a slave state. It was in Cincinnati that Harriet first became aware of the horrors of slavery.

Harriet and Calvin learned that their servant, Zillah, was actually a runaway slave. Calvin and Henry Ward Beecher drove her to the next station on the Underground Railroad. One night, Harriet's friend, Mr. Rankin, saw a young woman run across the Ohio River. It was winter. She was able to cross over the ice. She did it with a baby in her arms. This story moved Harriet deeply. It would later become one of the most famous scenes in *Uncle Tom's Cabin*.

In 1850, Professor Stowe joined the faculty of Bowdoin College. It was located in Brunswick, Maine. The Stowe family moved to Maine. They lived in Brunswick until 1853. In Brunswick, Harriet wrote her great book, *Uncle Tom's Cabin*. In it she dramatized the horrors of slavery. It was more intense and moving than all the abolitionist literature. The book was a great success. It changed the minds of a huge part of the population.

Abraham Lincoln met Harriet Beecher Stowe in 1862. He said, "So you're the little woman who wrote the book that started this Great War!"

"HARRIET BEECHER STOWE"
by Paul Laurence Dunbar

SHE told the story, and the whole world wept
At wrongs and cruelties it had not known
But for this fearless woman's voice alone.
She spoke to consciences that long had slept:
Her message, Freedom's clear reveille, swept
From heedless hovel to complacent throne.
Command and prophecy were in the tone,
And from its sheath the sword of justice leapt.
Around two peoples swelled a fiery wave,
But both came forth transfigured from the flame.
Blest be the hand that dared be strong to save,
And blest be she who in our weakness came—
Prophet and priestess! At one stroke she gave
A race to freedom and herself to fame.

1   Which of the following judgments can be made about how Harriet Beecher Stowe felt about slavery?

    A   She thought it was a way to build strength.
    B   She knew it was a necessary social evil.
    C   She felt it was a Southern tradition.
    D   She believed it was a great injustice.

2   The author *most* likely wrote this poem to—

    A   honor Stowe for writing *Uncle Tom's Cabin*
    B   explain why Stowe wrote *Uncle Tom's Cabin*
    C   analyze the events in *Uncle Tom's Cabin*
    D   describe the story of *Uncle Tom's Cabin*

3   The woman ran across the ice because she—

    A   was fleeing from slavery to a free state
    B   wanted to get hold of Mr. Rankin
    C   was looking for a doctor for her baby
    D   wanted to find Harriet Beecher Stowe

4   Which line from the poem is an example of personification?

    A   "She told the story, and the whole world wept"
    B   "But for this fearless woman's voice alone"
    C   "And from its sheath the sword of justice leapt"
    D   "A race to freedom and herself to fame"

     139

5 Do Abraham Lincoln and Paul Laurence Dunbar agree about Harriet Beecher Stowe? Be sure to write your response in your answer document.

_____

_____

_____

_____

_____

_____

_____

_____

_____

_____

_____

_____

_____

_____

_____

_____

_____

_____

_____

_____

_____

_____

_____

_____

_____

_____

Excerpted from "THE PIED PIPER OF HAMELIN, A CHILD'S STORY"

by Robert Browning

I.

Hamelin Town's in Brunswick,
By famous Hanover city;
The river Weser, deep and wide,
Washes its wall on the southern side
A pleasanter spot you never spied;
But, when begins my ditty,
Almost five hundred years ago,
To see the townsfolk suffer so
From vermin, was a pity.

II.

Rats!
They fought the dogs and killed the
    cats,
And bit the babies in the cradles,
And ate the cheeses out of the vats,
And licked the soup from the cook's
    own ladles.
Split open the kegs of salted sprats,
Made nests inside men's Sunday
    hats,
And even spoiled the women's chats
By drowning their speaking
With shrieking and squeaking
In fifty different sharps and flats.

III.

At last the people in a body
To the Town Hall came flocking:
" 'Tis clear," cried they, "our Mayor's
    a noddy;
And as for our Corporation—
    shocking
To think we buy gowns lined with
    ermine
For dolts that can't or won't
    determine
What's best to rid us of our vermin!
Rouse up, sirs! Give your brains a
    racking

To find the remedy we're lacking,
Or, sure as fate, we'll send you
    packing!"
At this the Mayor and Corporation
Quaked with a mighty
    consternation.

IV.

"Bless us," cried the Mayor, "what's
    that?"
(With the Corporation as he sat
Looking little though wondrous fat;
Nor brighter was his eye, nor
    moister
Than a too-long-opened oyster,
Save when at noon his paunch grew
    mutinous
For a plate of turtle green and
    glutinous),
"Only a scraping of shoes on the mat
Anything like the sound of a rat
Makes my heart go pit-a-pat!"

V.

"Come in!"—the Mayor cried,
    looking bigger:
And in did come the strangest
    figure!
His queer long coat from heel to
    head
Was half of yellow and half of red,
And he himself was tall and thin,
With sharp blue eyes, each like a
    pin,
And light loose hair, yet swarthy
    skin,
No tuft on cheek nor beard on chin,
But lips where smiles went out and
    in;
There was no guessing his kith and
    kin:

And nobody could enough admire
The tall man and his quaint attire.

VI.

He advanced to the council-table:
And, "Please your honors," said he,
    "I'm able,
By means of a secret charm, to draw
All creatures living beneath the sun,
That creep or swim or fly or run,
After me so as you never saw!
And I chiefly use my charm
On creatures that do people harm,
The mole and toad and newt and
    viper;
And people call me the Pied Piper."
(And here they noticed round his
    neck
A scarf of red and yellow stripe,
To match with his coat of the self-
    same cheque;
And at the scarf's end hung a pipe;
And his fingers, they noticed, were
    ever straying

As if impatient to be playing
Upon this pipe, as low it dangled
Over his vesture so old-fangled.)
"Yet," said he, "poor piper as I am,
In Tartary I freed the Cham,
Last June, from his huge swarms of
    gnats;
I eased in Asia the Nizam
Of a monstrous brood of vampyre-
    bats:
And as for what your brain
    bewilders,
If I can rid your town of rats
Will you give me a thousand
    guilders?"
"One? fifty thousand!"—was the
    exclamation
Of the astonished Mayor and
    Corporation.

1   Read the following lines from the poem and then answer the question.

"And I chiefly use my charm

On creatures that do people harm,

The mole and toad and newt and viper;

And people call me the Pied Piper."

The author probably chooses these words to show that the Pied Piper—

A   uses his power to rid people of pests
B   uses his power to hurt unkind people
C   uses animals to get back at people
D   uses people to make animals angry

142

2 Which word *best* describes the Mayor?

    A Reserved
    B Devoted
    C Focused
    D Worried

3 Which is the *best* summary for this poem?

    A Mayors run towns in different ways.
    B Rats come and take over the town.
    C A strange man comes to a town.
    D People dress oddly in the town.

4 Read the following line from the poem and then answer the question.

    "One? fifty thousand!"

Which of the following judgments can be made about why the Mayor says this line?

    A The Mayor will not hire the Pied Piper.
    B The Pied Piper does not like rats at all.
    C The Mayor wants the rats to be gone.
    D The Pied Piper asked for too much money.

5 Which word *best* describes the Pied Piper?

    A Mean and scary
    B Active and colorful
    C Pushy and forceful
    D Caring and generous

6 Read the following lines from the poem and then answer the question.

"And as for what your brain bewilders

If I can rid your town of rats

Will you give me a thousand guilders?"

The author probably chooses these words to show that—

A the rats are demanding to be paid before they leave town
B the Pied Piper is willing to pay someone to get rid of the rats
C the rats in the town are doing a lot of costly damage
D the Pied Piper wants to be paid for getting rid of the rats

7 The people *most* likely complained about the Mayor because—

A he had allowed the Pied Piper into town
B he had done nothing about the rat crisis
C he ate too much and left nothing for them
D he did not encourage his staff to do work

8 The author *most* likely includes the first stanza to—

A describe the scene
B explain that the story is made-up
C develop the problem
D introduce the characters

9 What do you think will happen next? Be sure to write your response in your answer document.

_____

_____

_____

_____

_____

_____

_____

_____

_____

_____

_____

_____

_____

_____

_____

_____

_____

_____

_____

_____

_____

_____

_____

_____

from "HIAWATHA'S CHILDHOOD"

by Henry Wadsworth Longfellow

By the shores of Gitche Gumee,
By the shining Big-Sea-Water,
Stood the wigwam of Nokomis,
Daughter of the moon, Nokomis.
Dark behind it rose the forest,
Rose the black and gloomy pine
   trees,
Rose the firs with cones upon them.
Bright before it beat the water,
Beat the clear and sunny water,
Beat the shining Big-Sea-Water.

There the wrinkled old Nokomis
Nursed the little Hiawatha,
Rocked him in his linden cradle,
Bedded soft in moss and rushes,
Safely bound with reindeer sinews;
Stilled his fretful wail by saying,
"Hush! the Naked Bear will hear
   thee!"
Lulled him into slumber, singing,
"Ewa-yea! my little owlet!
Who is this that lights the wigwam?
With his great eyes lights the
   wigwam?
Ewa-yea! my little owlet!"

Many things Nokomis taught him
Of the stars that shine in heaven;
Showed him Ishkoodah, the comet,
Ishkoodah with fiery tresses;
Showed the Death-Dance of the
   spirits,
Warriors with their plumes and war
   clubs,
Flaring far away to northward
In the frosty nights of winter;
Showed the broad white road in
   heaven,
Pathway of the ghosts, the shadows,
Running straight across the
   heavens,
Crowded with the ghosts, the
   shadows.

At the door on summer evenings
Sat the little Hiawatha;
Heard the whispering of the pine
   trees,
Heard the lapping of the waters,
Sounds of music, words of wonder;
"Minne-wawa" said the pine trees,
"Mudway-ashka!" said the water.

Saw the firefly, Wah-wah-taysee,
Flitting through the dusk of
   evening,
With the twinkle of its candle
Lighting up the brakes and bushes,
And he sang the song of children,
Sang the song Nokomis taught him:
"Wah-wah-taysee, little firefly,
Little, flitting, white-fire insect,
Little, dancing, white-fire creature,
Light me with your little candle,
Ere upon my bed I lay me,
Ere in sleep I close my eyelids!"

Saw the moon rise from the water,
Rippling, rounding from the water,
Saw the flecks and shadows on it,
Whispered, "What is that,
   Nokomis?"
And the good Nokomis answered:
"Once a warrior, very angry,
Seized his grandmother and threw
   her
Up into the sky at midnight;
Right against the moon he threw
   her.
'Tis her body that you see there."

Saw the rainbow in the heaven,
In the eastern sky, the rainbow,
Whispered, "What is that,
   Nokomis?"
And the good Nokomis answered:
" 'Tis the heaven of flowers you see
   there;

All the wild flowers of the forest,
All the lilies of the prairie,
When on earth they fade and perish,
Blossom in that heaven above us."

When he heard the owls at
    midnight,
Hooting, laughing, in the forest,
"What is that?" he cried in terror,
"What is that," he said, "Nokomis?"
And the good Nokomis answered.
"That is but the owl and owlet,
Talking in their native language,
Talking, scolding, at each other."

Then the little Hiawatha
Learned of every bird its language,
Learned their names and all their
    secrets,
How they built their nests in
    summer,
Where they hid themselves in
    winter,
Talked with them whene'er he met
    them,
Called them "Hiawatha's Chickens."

Of all beasts he learned the
    language,
Learned their names and all their
    secrets,
How the beavers built their lodges.
Where the squirrels hid their
    acorns,
How the reindeer ran so swiftly,
Why the rabbit was so timid,
Talked with them whene'er he met
    them,
Called them "Hiawatha's Brothers."

Then Iagoo the great boaster,
He the marvelous story-teller,
He the traveler and the talker,
He the friend of old Nokomis,
Made a bow for Hiawatha;
From a branch of ash he made it,
From an oak bough made the
    arrows,

Tipped with flint, and winged with
    feathers,
And the cord he made of deerskin.

Then he said to Hiawatha:
"Go, my son, into the forest,
Where the red deer herd together,
Kill for us a famous roebuck,
Kill for us a deer with antlers!"

Forth into the forest straightway
All alone walked Hiawatha
Proudly, with his bow and arrows;
And the birds sang round him, o'er
    him
"Do not shoot us, Hiawatha!"
Sang the robin, sang the bluebird,
"Do not shoot us, Hiawatha!"

And the rabbit from his pathway
Leaped aside, and at a distance
Sat erect upon his haunches,
Half in fear and half in frolic,
Saying to the little hunter,
"Do not shoot me, Hiawatha!"

But he heeded not, nor heard them,
For his thoughts were with the red
    deer;
On their tracks his eyes were
    fastened,
Leading downward to the river,
To the ford across the river,
And as one in slumber walked he.

Hidden in the alder bushes,
There he waited till the deer came,
Till he saw two antlers lifted,
Saw two eyes look from the thicket,
Saw two nostrils point to windward,
And a deer came down the pathway,
Flecked with leafy light and shadow.
And his heart within him fluttered
Trembled like the leaves above him,
Like the birch-leaf palpitated,
As the deer came down the pathway.

147

Then, upon one knee uprising,
Hiawatha aimed an arrow;
Scarce a twig moved with his motion,
Scarce a leaf was stirred or rustled,
But the wary roebuck darted,
Stamped with all his hoofs together,
Listened with one foot uplifted,
Leaped as if to meet the arrow;
Ah! the singing, fatal arrow,
Like a wasp it buzzed, and stung him!

Dead he lay there in the forest,
By the ford across the river;
Beat his timid heart no longer;
But the heart of Hiawatha
Throbbed and shouted and exulted,
As he bore the red deer homeward.

1   Which word *best* describes Hiawatha?

   A   Mature
   B   Curious
   C   Rebellious
   D   Unfriendly

2   Which of these *best* describes what scared Hiawatha?

   A   The fireflies
   B   The moon
   C   The owls
   D   The bunnies

3   Hiawatha's heart throbbed and shouted on his way home because—

   A   he was late to see Nokomis
   B   he was afraid of the owl
   C   he had killed his first deer
   D   he thought the deer was heavy

148

4   Which of these *best* describes Nokomis called a rainbow?

   A   Reflections from the water
   B   Where the forest animals sleep
   C   Reflections of the fireflies
   D   Where flowers go when they wilt

5   Nokomis taught Hiawatha to—

   A   read from big books
   B   respect the animals
   C   tell time from the stars
   D   cook and clean house

6   Which line from the poem is an example of a simile?

   A   "There he waited till the deer came"
   B   "Like a wasp it buzzed, and stung him"
   C   "And the birds sang round him, o'er him"
   D   "From a branch of ash he made it"

7 Why did Hiawatha hunt for a red deer? What does it mean? Be sure to write your response in your answer document.

_____

_____

_____

_____

_____

_____

_____

_____

_____

_____

_____

_____

_____

_____

_____

_____

_____

_____

_____

_____

_____

_____

_____

_____

_____

from "THE RIME OF THE ANCIENT MARINER"

by Samuel Taylor Coleridge

PART I

An ancient Mariner meeteth three Gallants bidden to a wedding-feast, and detaineth one.

It is an ancient Mariner,
And he stoppeth one of three.
'By thy long beard and glittering eye,
Now wherefore stopp'st thou me?

The Bridegroom's doors are opened
   wide,
And I am next of kin;
The guests are met, the feast is set:
May'st hear the merry din.'

He holds him with his skinny hand,
'There was a ship,' quoth he.
'Hold off! unhand me, grey-beard
   loon!'
Eftsoons his hand dropt he.

The Wedding-Guest is spell-bound by the eye of the old seafaring man, and constrained to hear his tale.

He holds him with his glittering
   eye—
The Wedding-Guest stood still,
And listens like a three years' child:
The Mariner hath his will.

The Wedding-Guest sat on a stone:
He cannot choose but hear;
And thus spake on that ancient man,
The bright-eyed Mariner.

The ship was cheered, the harbour
   cleared,
Merrily did we drop
Below the kirk, below the hill,
Below the lighthouse top.

The Mariner tells how the ship sailed southward with a good wind and fair weather, till it reached the Line.

The Sun came up upon the left,
Out of the sea came he!
And he shone bright, and on the
   right
Went down into the sea.

Higher and higher every day,
Till over the mast at noon—'
The Wedding-Guest here beat his
   breast,
For he heard the loud bassoon.

The Wedding-Guest heareth the bridal music; but the Mariner continueth his tale.

The bride hath paced into the hall,
Red as a rose is she;
Nodding their heads before her goes
The merry minstrelsy.

The Wedding-Guest he beat his
   breast,
Yet he cannot choose but hear;
And thus spake on that ancient man,
The bright-eyed Mariner.

The ship driven by a storm toward the South Pole.

'And now the STORM-BLAST came,
   and he
Was tyrannous and strong:
He struck with his o'ertaking wings,
And chased us south along.

With sloping masts and dipping
   prow,
As who pursued with yell and blow
Still treads the shadow of his foe,

And forward bends his head,
The ship drove fast, loud roared the
    blast,
The southward aye we fled.

And now there came both mist and
    snow,
And it grew wondrous cold:
And ice, mast-high, came floating by,
As green as emerald.

*The land of ice, and of fearful sounds
where no living thing was to be seen.*

And through the drifts the snowy
    clifts
Did send a dismal sheen:
Nor shapes of men nor beasts we
    ken—
The ice was all between.

The ice was here, the ice was there,
The ice was all around:
It cracked and growled, and roared
    and howled,
Like noises in a swound!

*Till a great sea-bird, called the
Albatross, came through the snow-
fog, and was received with great joy
and hospitality.*

At length did cross an Albatross,
Through the fog it came;
As if it had been a Christian soul,
We hailed it in God's name.

It ate the food it ne'er had eat,
And round and round it flew.
The ice did split with a thunder-fit;
The helmsman steered us through!

*And lo! the Albatross proveth a bird
of good omen, and followeth the ship
as it returned northward through fog
and floating ice.*

And a good south wind sprung up
    behind;
The Albatross did follow,
And every day, for food or play,
Came to the mariner's hollo!

In mist or cloud, on mast or shroud,
It perched for vespers nine;
Whiles all the night, through fog-
    smoke white,
Glimmered the white Moon-shine.'

*The ancient Mariner inhospitably
killeth the pious bird of good omen.*

'God save thee, ancient Mariner!
From the fiends, that *plague* thee
    thus!—
Why look'st thou so?'—With my
    crossbow
I shot the ALBATROSS.

PART II

The Sun now rose upon the right:
Out of the sea came he,
Still hid in mist, and on the left
Went down into the sea.

And the good south wind still blew
    behind,
But no sweet bird did follow,
Nor any day for food or play
Came to the mariners' hollo!

*His shipmates cry out against the
ancient Mariner, for killing the bird
of good luck.*

And I had done an hellish thing,
And it would work 'em woe:
For all averred, I had killed the bird
That made the breeze to blow.

Ah wretch! said they, the bird to
    slay,
That made the breeze to blow!

152

But when the fog cleared off, they justify the same, and thus make themselves accomplices in the crime.

Nor dim nor red, like God's own
   head,
The glorious Sun uprist :
Then all averred, I had killed the
   bird
That brought the fog and mist.
'Twas right, said they, such birds to
   slay,
That bring the fog and mist.

The fair breeze continues; the ship enters the Pacific Ocean, and sails northward, even till it reaches the Line.

The fair breeze blew, the white foam
   flew,
The furrow followed free;
We were the first that ever burst
Into that silent sea.

The ship hath been suddenly becalmed.

Down dropt the breeze, the sails
   dropt down,
'Twas sad as sad could be;
And we did speak only to break
The silence of the sea!

All in a hot and copper sky,
The bloody Sun, at noon,
Right up above the mast did stand,
No bigger than the Moon.

Day after day, day after day,
We stuck, nor breath nor motion;
As idle as a painted ship
Upon a painted ocean.

And the Albatross begins to be avenged.

Water, water, every where,
And all the boards did shrink;
Water, water, every where,
Nor any drop to drink.

The very deep did rot: O Christ!
That ever this should be!
Yea, slimy things did crawl with legs
Upon the slimy sea.

About, about, in reel and rout
The death-fires danced at night;
The water, like a witch's oils,
Burnt green, and blue and white.

153

1 Which of these *best* describes a theme of the poem?

   A Disturbing nature can cause great misfortune.
   B Sailing is always a dangerous occupation.
   C Good stories are always worth listening to.
   D Despair will always come to the bravest explorers.

2 What is the meaning of *plague* as used in the poem?

   A Watch
   B Haunt
   C Assist
   D Gather

3 Which of these *best* describes why the ship stopped moving?

   A The sailors did not want to leave.
   B The water was not deep enough.
   C The ship ran into the ground.
   D The wind stopped pushing the sails.

4 The Wedding Guest beat his breast because he—

   A was frightened of the Ancient Mariner
   B could not bear to leave the Ancient Mariner
   C did not like the music playing at the wedding
   D wanted the bride to know he was outside

5 Which of the following judgments can be made about the poem?

   A The water was too dirty to drink.
   B There was little water nearby.
   C The sailors couldn't reach the water.
   D The water was from the salty ocean.

6 Which word *best* describes the speaker at the end of the poem?

    A Interested
    B Angry
    C Impatient
    D Unconcerned

7 Which of these had the sailors reached when the sun was over the mast at noon?

    A The North Pole
    B The equator
    C England
    D The South Pole

8 Which of these *best* describes what the Albatross is a symbol of?

    A A happy marriage
    B Good luck at sea
    C Pain and anguish
    D An oncoming storm

9 The author *most* likely breaks up the poem with sections in bold and italics to—

    A help the reader understand his poem
    B let the wedding guest talk to the mariner
    C add more to the poem and make it longer
    D separate ship events from the wedding

10 What happens to the ship and sailors at the end of this poem? Be sure to write your response in your answer document.

_____

_____

_____

_____

_____

_____

_____

_____

_____

_____

_____

_____

_____

_____

_____

_____

_____

_____

_____

_____

_____

_____

"TWO MOODS FROM THE HILL"

by Ernest Benshimol

I. YOUTH

I LOVE to watch the world from here, for all
The numberless living portraits that are drawn
Upon the mind. Far over is the sea,
Fronting the sand, a few great yellow dunes,
A salt marsh stumbling after, rank and green,
With brackish gullies wandering in between,
All this from the hill.
And more: a clump of dwarfed and twisted cedars,
Sentinels over the marsh, and bright with the sun
A field of daisies wandering in the wind
As though a hidden serpent glided through,
A broken wall, a new-plowed field, and then
The dusty road and the abodes of men
Surrounding the hill.
How small the enclosure is wherein there lives
Each phase and passion of life, the distant sail
Dips in the limpid bosom of the sea,
From that far place to where in state the turf
Raises a throne for me upon the hill,
Each little love and lust of a living thing
Can thus be compassed in a rainbow ring
And seen from the hill.

II. AGE

Why did I build my cottage on a hill
Facing the sea?
Why did I plan each terraced lawn to slope
Down to the deep blue billowy breast of hope,
Surging and sweeping,
laughing and leaping,
Tumbling its garments of foam upon the shore,
Rustling the sands that know my step no more,
I should have found a valley, deep and still,
To shelter me.

There flows the river, and it seems asleep
So far away,
Yet I remember whip of wave and roar
Of wind that rose and smote against the oar,
Smote and retreated,
Proud but defeated,
While I rejoiced and rowed into the brine,

Drawing on wet and heavy-straining line
The great cod quivering from the deep
As counterplay.

What is the *solace* of these hills and vales
That rise and fall?
What is there glorious in the greenwood glen,
Or twittering thrush or wing of darting wren?
Give me the gusty,
Raucous and rusty
Call of the sea gull in the echoing sky,
The wild shriek of the winds that cannot die,
Give me the life that follows the bending sails,
Or none at all!

1 Which of these *best* describes the tone of the poem?

   A Jolly
   B Forgetful
   C Regretful
   D Careless

2 What is the meaning of *solace* as used in the poem?

   A Silence
   B Comfort
   C Movement
   D Beauty

3 Which of these *best* describes the attitude of the speaker in "Youth"?

   A He is very afraid of the sea.
   B He is uninterested in the sea.
   C He is not aware of the sea.
   D He loves the sea very much.

4 Why doesn't the poet like his view of the sea in "Age"? Be sure to write your response in your answer document.

_____

_____

_____

_____

_____

_____

_____

_____

_____

_____

_____

_____

_____

_____

_____

_____

_____

_____

_____

_____

_____

_____

_____

_____

"THE PLANTING OF THE APPLE TREE"

by William Cullen Bryant

Come, let us plant the apple tree.
Cleave the tough greensward with
    the spade;
Wide let its hollow bed be made;
There gently lay the roots, and there
Sift the dark mold with kindly care,
And press it o'er them tenderly,
As round the sleeping infant's feet
We softly fold the cradle sheet;
So plant we the apple tree.

What plant we in this apple tree?
Buds, which the breath of summer
    days
Shall lengthen into leafy sprays;
Boughs where the thrush, with
    crimson breast,
Shall haunt, and sing, and hide her
    nest;
We plant, upon the sunny lea,
A shadow for the noontide hour,
A shelter from the summer shower,
When we plant the apple tree.

What plant we in this apple tree?
Sweets for a hundred flowery
    springs,
To load the May wind's restless
    wings,
When, from the orchard row, he
    pours
Its fragrance through our open
    doors;
A world of blossoms for the bee,
Flowers for the sick girl's silent
    room,
For the glad infant sprigs of bloom,
We plant with the apple tree.

What plant we in this apple tree?
Fruits that shall swell in sunny
    June,
And redden in the August noon,
And drop, when gentle airs come by,

That fan the blue September sky,
While children come, with cries of
    glee,
And seek them where the fragrant
    grass
Betrays their bed to those who pass,
At the foot of the apple tree.

And when, above this apple tree,
The winter stars are quivering
    bright,
The winds go howling through the
    night,
Girls, whose young eyes o'erflow
    with mirth,
Shall peel its fruit by cottage hearth,
And guests in prouder homes shall
    see,
Heaped with the grape of Cintra's
    vine,
And golden orange of the line,
The fruit of the apple tree.

The fruitage of this apple tree,
Winds and our flag of stripe and star
Shall bear to coasts that lie afar,
Where men shall wonder at the
    view,
And ask in what fair groves they
    grew;
And *sojourners* beyond the sea
Shall think of childhood's careless
    day,
And long, long hours of summer
    play,
In the shade of the apple tree.

Each year shall give this apple tree
A broader flush of roseate bloom,
A deeper maze of verdurous gloom,
And loosen, when the frost-clouds
    lower,
The crisp brown leaves in thicker
    shower.

The years shall come and pass, but we
Shall hear no longer, where we lie,
The summer's songs, the autumn's sigh,
In the boughs of the apple tree.

And time shall waste this apple tree.
Oh, when its aged branches throw
Thin shadows on the ground below,
Shall fraud and force and iron will
Oppress the weak and helpless still?
What shall the tasks of mercy be,
Amid the toils, the strifes, the tears
Of those who live when length of years
Is wasting this apple tree?
"Who planted this old apple tree?"
The children of that distant day
Thus to some aged man shall say;
The gray-haired man shall answer them:
"A poet of the land was he,
Born in the rude but good old times;
'Tis said he made some quaint old rhymes
On planting the apple tree."

1   What is the meaning of *sojourners* as used in the poem?

   A   Waves
   B   Trees
   C   Winds
   D   Travelers

2   Read the following line from the poem and then answer the question.

     "a shadow for the noontide hour"

   The author probably chooses these words to mean—

   A   a place for birds to rest
   B   a home for small animals
   C   protection from weather
   D   shade from the sun

3 What is the *most* important thing the apple tree produces?

   A Flowers
   B Shade
   C Fragrance
   D Apples

4 Which of these *best* describes the tone of the poem?

   A Sorrowful
   B Hopeful
   B Irritated
   D Informative

5 The author *most* likely wrote the last stanza of this poem to show—

   A what happens when the tree grows old
   B how to make the tree continue to grow
   C other types of trees that can be planted
   D special things the apple tree can be used for

6 Who do you think planted the apple tree? What makes you think so? Be sure to write your response in your answer document.

_____

_____

_____

_____

_____

_____

_____

_____

_____

_____

_____

_____

_____

_____

_____

_____

_____

_____

_____

_____

_____

_____

_____

THE DELAWARE PEOPLE

The Delaware River was named after Lord de la Warr, the governor of the Jamestown colony. In turn, the people who lived along this river were named "DELAWARE." The name later came to be applied to almost all Lenape people.

In our language, which belongs to the Algonquian language family, we call ourselves "LENAPE." It means something like "The People." Our ancestors were among the first American Indians to come in contact with the Europeans (Dutch, English, & Swedish) in the early 1600s. As Delaware, we were called the "Grandfather" tribe because we were respected by other tribes as peacemakers. We settled disputes among rival tribes. We were also known for our fierceness and tenacity as warriors when we had to fight.

However, we preferred to choose a path of peace with the Europeans and other tribes. Many of the early treaties and land sales we signed with the Europeans were, in our people's minds, more like leases. We had no idea that land was something that could be sold. We believed that the land belonged to the Creator, we were only using it to shelter and feed their people.

4   When the poor, **bedraggled** people got off their ships after the long voyage and needed a place to live, we shared the land with them. They gave us a few token gifts for our people's kindness. In the mind of the Europeans these gifts were actually the purchase price for the land.

Our Delaware people signed the first American Indian treaty with the newly formed United States government on September 17, 1778. Nevertheless, through war and peace, our ancestors had to continue to give up their lands and move westward. We were forced to move first to Ohio, then to Indiana, Missouri, Kansas, and finally, to Indian Territory—now Oklahoma.

One small band of Delawares left our group in the late 1700s. Through different migrations, they are today located at Anadarko, Oklahoma. Small contingents of Delawares fled to Canada during a time of extreme persecution. Today they occupy two reserves in Ontario. They are: The Delaware Nation at Moraviantown and The Munsee-Delaware Nation.

164

1   The Delaware were known as the "Grandfather" tribe because they were

   A   lighthearted people who enjoyed telling stories.
   B   peaceful people who helped others solve problems.
   C   an ancient group that existed for thousands of years.
   D   a little-known group that disappeared long ago.

2   In paragraph 4, <u>bedraggled</u> means

   A   powerful.
   B   intimidating.
   C   beneficial.
   D   filthy.

3   The passage explains how the Delaware were forced from their homelands.

   • Explain how and why the Delaware were made to move.

   Use information from the article to support your response.

   _____

   _____

   _____

   _____

   _____

   _____

   _____

   _____

   _____

   _____

   _____

   _____

   _____

CAPTAIN KIDD ON RARITAN BAY

In the late 17th and early 18th centuries the waters between Sandy Hook and New York City were infested with pirates and French privateers. Many landing parties rowed to shore or up the creeks and rivers of Central Jersey, including Wales Creek, Matawan Creek, Waycake Creek, and others. The famous pirate Blackbeard attacked farmers and villages near what is Middletown today. Captain Morgan often visited the area as well. The Morgan section of Sayreville is said to have been named after relatives of the infamous pirate.

Politicians, businessmen, and shipowners were often either bribed by, or did business with the pirtaes. Because of this, many of these men protected the pirates. Many wealthy colonial families' fortunes began with the pirates. Many would either invest in pirate expeditions, or buy plundered goods at a discount and resell them at a large profit. Pirates were not only tolerated, but in many cases they were openly encouraged. The most famous pirate to ever trawl the Jersey waters was the notorious Captain Kidd.

Captain William Kidd was born around 1645 in Scotland and later became a resident of New York City. After commanding a privateer ship in a successful expedition in the Caribbean, he established himself as a wealthy and politically connected colonist. He married a wealthy Monmouth County widow. He traveled to England in 1695 in search of a commission in the Royal Navy. Failing to gain a command in the British Navy, he was persuaded by political associates and schemers to seek a privateering license. With backing from many of the leading men in England, Kidd was granted a license by the king to seize and capture French and pirate ships, and split the booty with the government and his backers.

4   In May, 1696, Captain Kidd set sail from England for New York City in his new ship, the *Adventure Galley*. On the way, much of his crew was impressed (**forcibly drafted**) by a British Navy warship. This forced Kidd to recruit a new crew when he arrived in New York. He had to pay them a larger share of the profit than he had expected. He promised the crew sixty percent of the booty taken but, unfortunately, he had already promised sixty percent to his backers. With this inauspicious start, Kidd left for the Red Sea to seek his fortune.

In the spring of 1697, the *Adventure Galley* arrived in the Red Sea. Kidd quickly forgot about his primary mission. He ignored various pirates he encountered. He even docked in the same ports with some, making no attempt to apprehend them, as he was required to by the license granted to him by the king. At first Kidd did try to keep to his promise to attack only French ships.

However, his crew quickly tired of allowing rich ships of other nationalities to pass unmolested. They attempted a mutiny. During this revolt Kidd killed a gunner, William Moore, with a blow to the head, using a bucket as a weapon. The crew backed down, but Kidd was forever changed by the incident. He began to attack ships no matter what their nationality or origin. He had officially become a pirate.

166

7   After attacking and capturing several ships, Kidd made his name in pirate lore with the capture of the *Quedah Merchant*. It was a fabulously rich Indian ship traveling with silks, guns, spices and gold. He split some of the booty with his crew. He then **scuttled** the *Adventure Galley*. He sailed for the Caribbean on the captured Indian vessel, now renamed the *Adventure Prize*. On arrival, Kidd learned that he been denounced as a pirate, and was wanted by the British government. After scuttling the ship, he purchased a small sloop and headed for Boston with a small crew. He hoped to take care of the problem.

On the way to Boston, Kidd stopped at various locations in New Jersey. He dropped anchor off the coast of Monmouth County in Raritan Bay. From there he sent landing parties ashore to both New Jersey and New York City to fix his "pirate problem" with the government by using his political connections and the proceeds of his captured booty. It was common practice for pirates to buy safety or pardons from corrupt colonial politicians. After bribing all the appropriate people, and hiding some of his treasure, Kidd left for Boston to meet with the governor.

Upon his arrival in Boston, Kidd was arrested by the new governor (a fairly honest man for his day) and imprisoned. He claimed to have hidden a treasure of forty thousand British pounds, but rumors at the time put his missing treasure at four hundred thousand pounds. Only ten thousand pounds was ever recovered. It was sent to England along with Kidd in early 1700.

In order to protect prominent backers and associates, Kidd was given a quick trial before the Admiralty Court, with limited evidence allowed by the court, and some evidence suppressed by the prosecution. He was found guilty of the murder of William Moore and of piracy, and was sentenced to be publicly hanged. Captain William Kidd maintained his innocence to the end. He promised to retrieve his treasure and give it to his backers and the government if only they would release him and give him a ship. Whether he was telling the truth, or just trying to save his neck, we will never know.

1   In the late 17th and early 18th centuries, piracy was often looked upon

    A with disdain.
    B with disgust.
    C with favor.
    D with indifference.

2 In paragraph 7, <u>scuttled</u> means

    A sunk.
    B given away.
    C taken over.
    D found.

3 Capt. Kidd was born in

    A New York.
    B Boston.
    C England.
    D Scotland.

4 What problem did Kidd face when he became a privateer?

    A He promised to give away more than he seized.
    B He could not find anyone with a fast enough ship.
    C He did not have enough backers to support him.
    D He needed a license that nobody would give him.

5 Why did Kidd's crew mutiny?

    A He was withholding their earnings.
    B They were ignoring the king's orders.
    C They wanted to attack more ships.
    D He was ignoring his primary mission.

6 Why did Kidd's crew stop their mutiny?

    A They learned England planned to arrest him.
    B They took control of the *Quedah Merchant*.
    C He promised that he would attack more ships.
    D He scared them when he killed someone.

7 Kidd was given a particularly quick trial

    A in order to deport him immediately.
    B in order to protect some his backers.
    C because the evidence against him was so abundant.
    D because public opinion had already convicted him.

8 In paragraph 4, why does the author put the words <u>forcibly drafted</u> in parentheses?

    A because they define the previous word
    B because they are not part of the story
    C because they are a quote from Kidd
    D because they are the name of a ship

9 This selection gives a lot of information about Captain Kidd.

    • What might lead one to believe that Captain Kidd had buried treasure?
    • Explain your reasoning.

Use information from the article to support your response.

_____

_____

_____

_____

_____

_____

_____

_____

_____

_____

_____

_____

_____

_____

_____

_____

169

WOODROW WILSON

Like Roosevelt before him, Woodrow Wilson regarded himself as the personal representative of the people. "No one but the president," he said, "seems to be expected . . . to look out for the general interests of the country." Wilson developed a program of progressive reform and asserted international leadership in building a new world order. In 1917, he proclaimed the American entrance into World War I a crusade to make the world "safe for democracy."

Wilson had seen the frightfulness of war. He was born in Virginia in 1856. He was the son of a Presbyterian minister. During the Civil War his father was a pastor in Augusta, Georgia. During Reconstruction, Wilson's father was a professor in the charred city of Columbia, South Carolina.

Wilson graduated from Princeton University (then the College of New Jersey) and wento on to the University of Virginia Law School. Wilson earned his doctorate at Johns Hopkins University. He entered upon a career in academics. In 1885 he married Ellen Louise Axson. Wilson advanced rapidly as a conservative young professor of political science. He became president of Princeton in 1902.

4   His growing national reputation led some conservative Democrats to consider him presidential timber. They persuaded him to run for governor of New Jersey in 1910. **In the campaign he asserted his independence of the conservatives and of the <u>machine</u> that had nominated him**. He endorsed a progressive platform, which he pursued as governor.

He was nominated for president at the 1912 Democratic convention. He campaigned on a program called the "New Freedom." It stressed individualism and states' rights. In the three-way election he received an overwhelming electoral vote, but only forty-two percent of the popular vote.

As president, Wilson maneuvered three major pieces of legislation through Congress. The first was a lower tariff, the Underwood Act; attached to the measure was a graduated federal income tax. The passage of the Federal Reserve Act provided the nation with the more elastic money supply it badly needed. In 1914 antitrust legislation established a Federal Trade Commission to prohibit unfair business practices.

Another burst of legislation followed in 1916. One new law prohibited child labor. Another limited railroad workers to an eight-hour day. By virtue of this legislation and the slogan, "he kept us out of war," Wilson narrowly won reelection. After the election however, Wilson concluded that America could not remain neutral in the World War. On April 2, 1917, he asked Congress for a declaration of war on Germany.

8   Massive American effort slowly tipped the balance in favor of the Allies. Wilson went before Congress in January, 1918, to **enunciate** American war aims. He listed Fourteen Points, the last of which would establish "A general association of nations . . . affording mutual guarantees of political independence and territorial integrity to great and small states alike."

After the Germans signed the Armistice in November, 1918, Wilson went to Paris to try to build an enduring peace. He later presented the Senate with the Versailles Treaty, containing the Covenant of the League of Nations. Wilson asked, "Dare we reject it and break the heart of the world?"

The election of 1918 had shifted the balance in Congress to the Republicans. By seven votes the Versailles Treaty failed in the Senate. The president, against the warnings of his doctors, had made a national tour to mobilize public sentiment for the treaty. Exhausted, he suffered a stroke and nearly died. Tenderly nursed by his second wife, Edith Bolling Galt, Woodrow Wilson lived until 1924.

1   Wilson first learned about the frightfulness of war when he

    A   served in the army in the Spanish-American War.
    B   served as American president during World War I.
    C   lived in the South during and after the Civil War.
    D   met veterans who served in the War of 1812.

2   In paragraph 4, Wilson "asserted his independence of the conservatives and of the machine that had nominated him." What is the meaning of <u>machine</u> in this article?

    A   an item that performs a specific task
    B   an organization of political people
    C   a large and fast vehicle or automobile
    D   a bank device that dispenses money

3   In which state did Woodrow Wilson go to college?

    A   Virginia
    B   Georgia
    C   South Carolina
    D   New Jersey

4 According to the article, which country did the United States fight against in World War I?

    A Great Britain
    B Japan
    C Italy
    D Germany

5 Which of the following accomplishments took place first in Wilson's life?

    A named president of Princeton
    B elected governor of New Jersey
    C promoted the League of Nations
    D established child labor laws

6 In paragraph 8, the author writes, "Wilson went before Congress in January, 1918, to enunciate American war aims." What is the meaning of enunciate?

    A to define in a statement
    B to pronounce carefully
    C to plead for more help
    D to give up and surrender

7 In which year was Woodrow Wilson first elected president?

    A 1902
    B 1910
    C 1912
    D 1916

8 Why did the Treaty of Versailles most likely fail in the Senate?

    A Woodrow Wilson did not tour until after it was voted on.
    B Woodrow Wilson almost died when he had a bad strike.
    C Woodrow Wilson campaigned fiercely against the treaty.
    D Woodrow Wilson's political party lost control of Congress.

9   Woodrow Wilson lived a life full of important deeds.

- Which of Wilson's accomplishments do you think was best?
- Which of Wilson's failures do you think was worst?

Use information from the article to support your answer.

_____

_____

_____

_____

_____

_____

_____

_____

_____

_____

_____

_____

_____

_____

_____

_____

_____

_____

_____

_____

173

VALLEY FORGE

General George Washington's winter quarters at Valley Forge were only twenty miles from Philadelphia. It is matter for wonder that the British general, William Howe, with a well-equipped army, did not make some attempt to destroy the army of Washington which passed the winter nearby and in acute distress. The Pennsylvania Loyalists, with dark days soon to come, were bitter at Howe's inactivity. There was a time when, in Washington's whole force, not more than two thousand men were in a condition to fight.

Congress was responsible for the needs of the army. It was now, in sordid inefficiency, cooped up in the little town of York, eighty miles west of Valley Forge, to which it had fled. There was as yet no real federal union. The seat of authority was in the state governments. Congress rapidly declined in public esteem. "What a lot of damned scoundrels we had in that second Congress," said, at a later date, Gouverneur Morris of Philadelphia to John Jay of New York, and Jay answered gravely, "Yes, we had." The body, so despised in retrospect, had no real executive government, no organized departments.

Already before independence was proclaimed there had been talk of a permanent union. The members of Congress had shown no sense of urgency. It was not until November 15, 1777, when the British were in Philadelphia and Congress was in exile at York, that the *Articles of Confederation* were adopted. By the following midsummer many of the states had ratified these articles. Maryland, the last to <u>assent</u>, did not accept the new union until 1781. Congress continued to act for the states without constitutional sanction during the greater part of the war.

Inefficiency, meanwhile, brought terrible suffering at Valley Forge. The horrors of that winter still remain vivid in the memory of the American people. The army marched to Valley Forge on December 17, 1777. In midwinter everything from houses to entrenchments still had to be created. At once there was busy activity in cutting down trees for the log huts. They were built nearly square, sixteen feet by fourteen, in rows, with the door opening on improvised streets.

Since boards were scarce and it was difficult to make roofs rainproof, Washington tried to stimulate ingenuity by offering a reward of one hundred dollars for an improved method of roofing. The fireplaces of wood were protected with thick clay. Firewood was abundant, but with little food for oxen and horses, men had to turn themselves into draught animals to bring in supplies.

Sometimes the army was without meat for a week. Many horses died for lack of forage or of proper care, a waste that especially disturbed Washington, a lover of horses. When quantities of clothing were ready for use, they were not delivered at Valley Forge owing to lack of transport. Washington expressed his contempt for officers who resigned their commissions in the face of these distresses. No one, he told them, had ever heard him say a word about resignation.

There were many desertions, but on the whole he marveled at the patience of his men and the fact that they did not mutiny. With a certain grim humor, they chanted phrases about "no pay, no clothes, no provisions, no rum," and sang an ode glorifying war and Washington. Hundreds of them marched barefoot, their blood staining the snow or the frozen ground while, at the same time, stores of shoes and clothing were lying unused somewhere on the roads to the camp.

Sickness raged in the army. Few men at Valley Forge, wrote Washington, had more than a sheet, many only part of a sheet, and some had nothing at all. Hospital stores were lacking. For want of straw and blankets the sick lay perishing on the frozen ground. When Washington had been at Valley Forge for less than a week, he had to report nearly three thousand men unfit for duty because of their nakedness in the bitter winter. Then, as always, what we now call the "profiteer" was holding up supplies for higher prices. To the British at Philadelphia, because they paid in gold, things were furnished which were denied to Washington at Valley Forge. He announced that he would hang anyone who took provisions to Philadelphia.

To keep his men alive, Washington had sometimes to take food by force from the inhabitants. With many sick, his horses so disabled that he could not move his artillery, and his defenses very slight, he could have made only a weak fight had Howe attacked him. Yet the legislature of Pennsylvania told him that, instead of lying quiet in winter quarters, he ought to be carrying on an active campaign. In most wars irresponsible men sitting by comfortable firesides are sure that they know best how the thing should be done.

1 According to the passage, the *Articles of Confederation* were created to

   A unite the colonies.
   B declare America's independence.
   C form the third Congress.
   D put Congress in charge of the army.

2 According to the passage, what is the primary reason that the men at Valley Forge had to haul all of the materials and supplies?

   A They had been forced to eat all of the animals.
   B Congress could not supply them with any animals.
   C The animals were too weak to carry the supplies.
   D The horses and oxen had run away from the camp.

3 As used in the passage, what does the word <u>assent</u> mean?

   A climb
   B challenge
   C agree to
   D sign

4 Washington offered a monetary reward to anyone who could

    A find a way to feed the horses.
    B build a cabin without using wood.
    C transport shoes to Valley Forge.
    D make a roof that did not leak.

5 Which line from the passage is an example of imagery?

    A "Many horses died for lack of forage or of proper care"
    B "Hundreds of them marched barefoot, their blood staining the snow"
    C "Congress continued to act for the states without constitutional sanction"
    D "before independence was proclaimed there had been talk of a permanent union"

6 Why does the writer most likely refer to the men in the Pennsylvania legislature as "irresponsible men sitting by comfortable firesides"?

    A to prove that they had never fought in a war before
    B to illustrate that they knew so much about fighting wars
    C to criticize them for failing to help Washington
    D to show that conditions at Valley Forge weren't really that bad

7 According to the passage, which of these is the most likely reason that Washington sometimes took food by force from the inhabitants of the town of Valley Forge?

    A He wanted to call attention to the problems there.
    B His men hoped to take over the people's homes.
    C He wanted to scare the local people into helping the army.
    D His men were on the verge of starvation.

8 Why do you think that General Howe did not attack Washington at Valley Forge? Use examples from the passage to support your response.

_____

_____

_____

_____

_____

_____

_____

_____

_____

_____

9 Who was most to blame for the suffering at Valley Forge? Use examples from the passage to support your response.

_____

_____

_____

_____

_____

_____

_____

_____

_____

_____

_____

_____

_____

THE BATTLE OF GETTYSBURG – Part I
JUNE 30TH–JULY 1ST

Gettysburg was, first of all, an act of fate. It was a three-day holocaust, largely unplanned and uncontrollable. Like the war itself, it sprang from decisions that men under pressure made in the light of imperfect knowledge. It would someday symbolize the war with all the blunders and heroism, hopes and delusions, combativeness and blinding devotion. With its enormous destruction, tactical maneuvers, and use of weapons, Gettysburg was one of the most dramatic and most typical of the 2,000-odd land engagements of the Civil War.

After the great victory at Chancellorsville, the Confederate cause in the eastern theater looked exceptionally bright. If 60,000 men could beat 134,000, then the Confederacy's inferiority in manpower would not determine the outcome of the war. It was surely offset by superior generalship and skill at arms. If the Confederate president, Jefferson Davis, and General Robert E. Lee were overly <u>optimistic</u>, they could hardly be blamed. Both men favored another invasion of the North. Lee made ready to move into Pennsylvania. In early June, Lee began moving his units away from Fredericksburg.

The Federals learned that Confederate infantrymen were west of the Blue Ridge heading north. General Joseph Hooker started to move to protect Washington and Baltimore. Earlier, President Abraham Lincoln had vetoed Hooker's proposal to seize Richmond while Lee went north. As the Confederate Army of Northern Virginia moved through the valleys and deployed into Pennsylvania behind cavalry screens, the Union Army of the Potomac moved north on a broad front to the east.

Outposts of both armies clashed during the afternoon of June 30th near the quiet little Pennsylvania market town of Gettysburg. The terrain in the area included rolling hills and broad shallow valleys. Gettysburg was the junction of twelve roads that led to Harrisburg, Philadelphia, Baltimore, Washington, and the mountain passes to the west, which were controlled by Lee. The rest was inevitable. The local commanders sent reports and recommendations to their superiors, who relayed them upward. Both armies, still widely dispersed, started moving toward Gettysburg.

On July 1st, Union cavalrymen fought a dismounted delaying action against advance troops of Lieutenant General Ambrose P. Hill's corps northwest of town. By this stage of the war, cavalrymen—armed with saber, pistol, and breech-loading carbine—were often deployed as mounted infantrymen, riding to battle but fighting on foot. The range and accuracy of the infantry's rifled muskets made it next to impossible for mounted men to attack foot soldiers in position. With their superior speed and mobility, cavalrymen, as witnessed in the Gettysburg campaign, were especially useful for screening, reconnaissance, and advance guard actions. They seized and held important hills, river crossings, and road junctions pending the arrival of infantry. During the morning hours of July 1st, this was the role played by Union horsemen on the ridges north and west of Gettysburg.

178

By noon, both the I and the XI Corps of the Army of the Potomac had joined in the battle. Lieutenant General Richard S. Ewell's Corps of Confederates had moved to support Hill. The latter, advancing from the north, broke the lines of the XI Corps. They drove the Federals back through Gettysburg. The Union infantry rallied behind artillery positioned on Cemetery and Culp's Hills south of the town. Lee reached the field about 2:00 p.m. He ordered Ewell to take Cemetery Hill, "if possible." However, Ewell failed to press his advantage. The Confederates settled into positions extending in a great curve from northeast of Culp's Hill, westward through Gettysburg, thence south on Seminary Ridge. During the night the Federals, enjoying interior lines, moved troops onto the key points of Culp's Hill, Cemetery Hill, Cemetery Ridge, and Little Round Top.

1   What is the main point of the passage's first paragraph?

   A   The battle at Gettysburg was not important to the outcome of the war.
   B   The Federals were losing all hope of winning the war.
   C   The battle at Gettysburg had not been planned by either of the two armies.
   D   The Confederates were greatly outnumbered in battle.

2   As used in the passage, what does the word optimistic mean?

   A   confident
   B   interested
   C   drained
   D   grateful

3   According to the passage, why were the Confederates hopeful before the Battle of Gettysburg?

   A   General Hooker had seized Richmond while Lee went north.
   B   General Lee was from Pennsylvania and knew the area well.
   C   They believed that their leadership and skill would help them to win.
   D   They knew that they would soon be getting many more soldiers.

4   Which statement about the area around Gettysburg is supported by the passage?

   A   It was one long, wide plain.
   B   It was made up of hills and valleys.
   C   It was made up of streams and rivers.
   D   It was a new, urban community.

5   According to the passage, why was the town of Gettysburg considered to be a strategic location?

    A   Gettysburg was a very large city.
    B   Gettysburg had many markets.
    C   Gettysburg was the site of a major junction.
    D   Gettysburg had many train stations.

6   During the Battle of Gettysburg, what were cavalry units used for?

    A   to attack artillery positions on the tops of hills
    B   to defend against ground infantry attacks in the valleys
    C   to hold important positions until the infantry arrived
    D   to make assaults on foot soldiers positioned defensively

7   According to the passage, what was one advantage that the Federals had in the Battle of Gettysburg?

    A   They had the element of surprise.
    B   They arrived there first.
    C   Their lines formed a large curve.
    D   They had interior lines.

THE BATTLE OF GETTYSBURG – Part II
JULY 3RD

General George Gordon Meade, after requesting the opinions of his corps commanders, decided to defend, rather than attack, on July 3rd. He also estimated that General Robert E. Lee, having attacked his right and left, would try for his center. He was right. Lee had planned to launch a full-scale, coordinated attack all along the line. He then changed his mind in favor of a massive frontal assault. It was to be made by ten brigades from four divisions of Longstreet's and Hill's corps against the Union center. The center was held by Major General Winfield Scott Hancock's II Corps. The assault was to be preceded by a massive artillery barrage.

At 1:00 p.m. on July 3rd, Confederate gunners opened fire from approximately 140 pieces along Seminary Ridge. It was the greatest artillery bombardment witnessed on the American continent up to that time. For two hours the barrage continued. It did little more than tear up ground, destroy a few caissons, and <u>expend</u> ammunition. The Union artillery in the sector, numbering only 80 guns, had not been knocked out. It did stop firing in order to conserve ammunition. The silence seemed to be a signal that the Confederates should begin their attack.

Under command of Major General George E. Pickett, 15,000 men emerged from the woods on Seminary Ridge. They were dressed as if on parade. They began the mile-long, 20-minute march toward Cemetery Ridge. The assault force—47 regiments altogether—moved at a walk until it neared the Union lines. Then it broke into a run. Union artillery, especially 40 Napoleons on the south end of the ridge and some rifled guns on Little Round Top, opened fire. Despite heavy casualties, the Confederates kept their formation until they came within rifle and canister range of the II Corps. By then the lines and units were intermingled. The four brigades composing the left of Pickett's first line were heavily hit, but actually reached and crossed the stone wall defended by Brigadier General John Gibbon's division, only to be quickly cut down or captured. Pickett's survivors withdrew to Seminary Ridge. The fighting was over except for a suicidal mounted charge by Union cavalry, which Longstreet's right flank units easily halted.

Both sides had fought hard and with great valor. Among 90,000 effective Union troops and 75,000 Confederates, there were more than 51,000 casualties. The Union Army of the Potomac lost 3,155 killed, 14,529 wounded, and 5,365 imprisoned and missing. Of the Confederate Army of Northern Virginia, 3,903 were killed, 18,735 wounded, and 5,425 missing and imprisoned.

If Chancellorsville was Lee's finest battle, Gettysburg was clearly his worst; yet the reverse did not unnerve him or reduce his effectiveness as a commander. The invasion had patently failed and he retired at once toward the Potomac. As that river was flooded, it was several days before he was able to cross. Mr. Lincoln, naturally pleased over Meade's defensive victory and elated over General Ulysses S. Grant's capture of Vicksburg, thought the war could end in 1863 if Meade launched a resolute pursuit and destroyed Lee's army on the north bank of the Potomac. However, Meade's own army was too mangled. The

Union commander moved cautiously, permitting Lee to return safely to Virginia on July 13th.

Gettysburg was the last important action in the eastern theater in 1863. Lee and Meade maneuvered against each other in Virginia, but there was no more fighting. After Gettysburg and Vicksburg the center of strategic gravity shifted to Tennessee.

1   According to the passage, Lee had originally planned to attack

   A   from the left and right flanks.
   B   all along the line.
   C   only if the Union attacked first.
   D   from the rear.

2   According to the passage, the Confederate artillery barrage

   A   was not at all successful.
   B   silenced the Union guns.
   C   weakened the Union lines.
   D   had not been planned beforehand.

3   As used in the passage, what does the word expend mean?

   A   wind up
   B   hold up
   C   use up
   D   make up

4   According to the passage, why did it take Lee three days to cross the Potomac River?

   A   The river was too wide.
   B   The river was at flood stage.
   C   He was hiding from General Meade.
   D   He was waiting for reinforcements.

5 What do you think would have happened if Meade had attacked Lee before he crossed the Potomac?

_____

_____

_____

_____

_____

_____

_____

_____

_____

_____

_____

_____

_____

_____

_____

_____

_____

DISPUTES OVER THE PENNS' PROPRIETORSHIP

The Presbyterians opposed the change to a royal governor. They believed that it would be followed by the establishment by law of the Church of England, with bishops and all the other ancient evils. They were well content with their position under the proprietors. They saw nothing to be gained under a royal governor.

One of the most striking instances of a change of sides was the case of a Philadelphia Quaker, John Dickinson. He was a lawyer with a large practice. He had wealth and position. He displayed not a little colonial magnificence when he drove in his coach and four. He was a member of the assembly. He had been in politics for some years. However, on this question of a change to royal government, he left the Quaker majority. He opposed the change with all his influence and ability. He and his father-in-law, Isaac Norris, Speaker of the Assembly, became the leaders against the change. Benjamin Franklin and Joseph Galloway, the latter afterwards a prominent Loyalist in the Revolution, were the leading <u>advocates</u> for the change.

The whole subject was thoroughly <u>thrashed out</u> in debates in the Assembly and in pamphlets. It must be remembered that this was the year 1764. It was on the eve of the American Revolution. British statesmen were planning a system of more rigorous control of the colonies. The advisability of a stamp tax was under consideration. Information about all these possible changes had reached the colonies. Dickinson foresaw the end and warned the people. Franklin and the Quaker party thought that there was no danger. They believed that the mother country could be implicitly trusted.

Dickinson warned the people that the British Ministry was starting special regulations for new colonies and "designing the strictest reformations in the old." It would be a great relief, he admitted, to be rid of the pettiness of the proprietors. It might be accomplished some time in the future, but not now. The proprietary system might be bad, but a royal government might be worse. It might wreck all the liberties of the province—religious freedom, the Assembly's control of its own adjournments, and its power of raising and disposing of the public money.

The ministry of the day in England was well known not to be favorably inclined towards Pennsylvania because of the frequently reported willfulness of the assembly, on which the recent disturbances had also been blamed. If the king, Ministry, and Parliament started upon a change, they might decide to reconstitute the assembly entirely, abolish its ancient privileges, and disfranchise both Quakers and Presbyterians.

The arguments of Franklin and Galloway consisted principally of assertions about the good intentions of the mother country and the absurdity of any fear on the part of the colonists for their privileges. But the king in whom they had so much confidence was George III. The Parliament that they thought would do no harm was the same one that a few months afterwards passed the Stamp Act, which eventually brought on the Revolution. Franklin and Galloway also asserted that the colonies like Massachusetts, the Jerseys, and the Carolinas, which had been changed to royal governments, had profited by the change.

184

However, that was hardly the prevailing opinion in those colonies themselves. Royal governors could be as petty and annoying as the Penns and far more tyrannical. Pennsylvania had always defeated any attempts at despotism on the part of the Penn family and had built up a splendid body of liberal laws and legislative privileges. Nevertheless, governors with the authority and power of the British Crown behind them could not be so easily resisted as the deputy governors of the Penns.

The assembly voted to appeal to England for the change. It appointed Franklin to be their agent before the Crown and Ministry. He sailed for England. He was soon involved in the opening scenes of the American Revolution. He was made the agent for all the colonies.

As for the assembly's petition for a change to royal government, Franklin presented it, but never pressed it. He, too, was finally convinced that the time was inopportune. In fact, the assembly itself before long began to have doubts and fears. It sent him word to let the subject drop. Amid much greater events, it was soon entirely forgotten.

1 Based on the passage, Presbyterians supported retaining the proprietary system of government because they

   A did not have to pay high taxes under the proprietary system.
   B believed that a royal governor would make them serve in the militia.
   C thought that the Quakers would become too powerful.
   D feared that they would be forced to join the Church of England.

2 Which would be the **best** alternative title for this passage?

   A "Not the Best Time for Change"
   B "A Powerful Assembly"
   C "Powerful Pennsylvania"
   D "Franklin and Galloway"

3 As used in the passage, what does the word <u>advocates</u> mean?

   A politicians
   B supporters
   C documents
   D systems

185

4 According to the passage, which of the following was an argument used in support of changing the government?

    A The assembly was ineffective.
    B The Penn family had taken away some of the colonists' rights.
    C The Stamp Tax would be beneficial to Pennsylvania.
    D Other colonies had benefited from making this change.

5 As used in the passage, what do the words <u>thrashed out</u> mean?

    A injured
    B researched
    C discussed
    D moved

6 Based on the end of the passage, Benjamin Franklin can **best** be described as

    A confident.
    B uncertain.
    C confused.
    D unhappy.

7 Based on the passage, John Dickinson was all of the following except

    A a Quaker.
    B a Loyalist.
    C a lawyer.
    D wealthy.

8 Based on the passage, the government of Pennsylvania did **not** change because

    A the assembly was unable to agree on what to do.
    B the king was opposed to such a move.
    C the assembly changed its mind about petitioning for a change.
    D Benjamin Franklin was unable to meet with the British government.

9 What did you find surprising about this passage? Why?

_____

_____

_____

_____

_____

_____

_____

_____

_____

_____

_____

_____

187

Made in the USA
Monee, IL
20 July 2020